SAGES AND SCHOOLMEN

by Arland Ussher
THE TWENTY TWO KEYS OF THE TAROT

★

by Arland Ussher and Carl von Metzradt
ENTER THESE ENCHANTED WOODS

ARLAND USSHER

Sages & Schoolmen

DUFOUR EDITIONS

*Set in Plantin type and printed in the Republic of
Ireland by Hely Thom Limited for
Dufour Editions Inc.
Chester Springs, Pennsylvania*

Library of Congress Catalog Card No. 66/29650

© *1967, Arland Ussher*

Contents

	page
Pythagoreans	7
Parmenides	9
Heraclitus	11
Empedocles	13
Anaxagoras	15
Democritus	16
Socrates	18
Plato	20
Protagoras	23
Aristotle	24
Stoics	27
Epicureans	29
Philo and Apollonius	32
Clement of Alexandria	33
Tertullian	35
Origen	37
Plotinus	39
Augustine	42
Boethius	45
John Scotus (Erigena)	46
Anselm	49
Abélard	51
Joachim of Flore	54
Arabians and Jews	56
Roger Bacon	58
Bonaventure	60
Thomas Aquinas	62
Duns Scotus	66
Eckhart	69

Sages & Schoolmen

Pythagoreans

THE HISTORY of philosophy, like that of art, may be represented as a single throw of a net or lasso—a net thrown to seize the Object, the ever appearing, changing and disappearing, Fact; philosophy begins and ends in Pattern—the pattern of the net, the pattern of the arrested, partially-held, Reality. The Pythagorean weaves, at one end of the European story—the Hegelian at the other end unweaves—the deterministic web of number and harmony; and the whole turbulent effort of our Western Reason and Will lies between them. For the Pythagorean, name and number still reside animistically in nature; they have not yet been separated off, like the Chorus from the Tragedy, into Plato's ideal Olympus; they and not we are the actors, or the dancers. The image is not yet the prisoners' Cavern, but the blacksmith's Forge, where the merry din of the rising and falling hammers is too continuous to be heard by the ears which have never known silence. The Pythagoreans' 'Tables of Correspondences', their squares and pentagrams, were later to become the stock-in-trade of the 'magus'. In those later days when philosophy had advanced to cope with the problems of the Self and the Not-Self, of volition and cognition, of (in short) religion and science—the aesthetic intuitions of the early ages survived only as bogus-religion and bogus-science, a 'secret lore' preserved by the ignorant and the base. Today, when religion and science themselves would appear to be either moribund or debased by the crowd, these intuitions can give us, if we will let them, what they gave to the disciples of Pythagoras—a pure joy of the mind, of similar nature to the joy we derive from music or from archaic linear art. A popular writer heaps ridicule on the statement—in

Plato's Pythagorean book the Timaeus—that the figure of Water is the equilateral triangle, the figure of Fire the isosceles triangle, the figure of Air the scalene triangle. Such a remark would seem to us an interesting and suggestive one if we were to come upon it in the note-book of a Cubist; for we should then approach it with the contemplative brooding attitude of the true philosopher, and leave behind us the niggling objections of the fact-bound reason. Nothing seems more preposterous to many modern minds than the Pythagorean beliefs, which for long hindered accurate research in astronomy, that the circle is the 'perfect figure'—and therefore the planets must move in circles—or that the number 10 is the 'perfect number'—for which reason an imaginary 'Anti-Earth' had to be included among the heavenly bodies, a notion later demolished by Aristotle. Certainly it is the task of a truly critical philosophy to be ever on the alert to distinguish between symbolism and science. But the truth that imperfection is necessary to perfection, or number to unity, is nevertheless well illustrated by the circle, in which the straight line of the Will bends into a curve only to return on itself—by the alternation of the 'male' Odd and the 'female' Even in counting—or by the manner in which the Monad loses itself in the Triad, thrice-repeated, and recovers itself in the Decad. The Pythagorean identifications of the Point with Unity, the Line with Duality, the Plane with Trinity, and the Solid with Quaternity are of wide metaphysical import, and are suggested (it is impossible not to think) even in the etymology of the Teutonic languages. *One* is *In*, the potentiality of this world of forms hidden within eternity, as within a point of no magnitude; *Two* is *To*, a first activity, a *tensed* or temporal energy, proceeding in a straight line; *Three* is *Through*, the sound of the tongue placed between the *twoness* of the *teeth*, the crossing of Force by Force in the spatial field—in a word, the plane; *Four* is *For*, the solid Object, entity and end of all thought and striving (again identified by Pythagoras with Justice)—it is also *Fire*, the drying of Matter by its internal tensions, in which it breaks and gives birth to the 'Quintessence', Life, like a soul released from its prison in the inanimate. On the other hand, the mysterious properties of irrational quantities appalled the Pythagoreans;

those who divulged them came, it was said, to violent deaths. They were perhaps in this like children who see a face in the pattern of a wall-paper—it was the face that would one day set fire to the old civilisation, the revenge of the despised 'Even' (the Unformed) upon the 'Odd' (the Formed). The same dreaded Irrational Principle was the fallacy in their logically-perfect theory of Eternal Recurrence; the moderns have discovered in this world hiding-crannies of the Will which the philosophers of determinism, with their hope of an 'Escape from the Wheel of Births', never dreamed of. Was it a presentiment of that solitude of the soul which made the Greeks exalt the friendship of man and man, like a shield, higher than it has ever been exalted—and which has left us the noble legend of the Pythagorean twain, Damon and Pythias?

Parmenides

THE PYTHAGOREAN doctrine of Numbers led quickly and naturally to the question 'How can Number be?'—or in other words 'How, from One, can come Two?' It is that *pons asinorum* of theology as well as of philosophy 'How could Perfect Reason create the daemon of Change, necessary to every act of creation as much as of destruction?' For Change must imply some insufficiency. In this dilemma there are (as, logically and gramatically, there are in all logical dilemmas) but two alternatives open. The first is the answer given by Democritus, and in general by the pluralists and mechanists, that Everything is Accident; in which case that belief is itself an accident, and not necessarily true or false or a third thing (for this strictly-unthinkable argument does not exclude, but rather involves, an 'Excluded Middle'). The second is the—more rationally watertight but at first sight more monstrous—theory of the monists, among whom Parmenides is the earliest great secular name, that the world of movement and multiplicity is an illusion. Christian mystics have sought to soften the monstrosity, in the only manner possible, by a paradox;

suggesting that without that spatio-temporal looking-glass of Illusion, Truth could not know itself for or truly *be* Truth—that in short Unity would then be but a Zero. But here we anticipate, for neither Parmenides nor his contemporary Gautama Buddha saw so far as this. The importance of the Eleatics is that, while believing in the space-continuum as a quasi-physical crystal mirror, they maintained—not merely by intuition and dogma but by some excellent arguments—that we live among shadows and distortions. In them, Reason—which creates the world of objects—proceeded to destroy that world, and was able to do so just because of the flaw of irrationality in creation. The puzzles propounded by Zeno in respect to number and motion do not need re-telling here; their refutation is as simple—and as inconclusive—as Johnson's refutation of Berkeley when he kicked the stone. Viewed under the aspect of Eternity, Achilles does not in fact overtake the tortoise; in the fine saying of T. S. Eliot, 'Time does not heal, the patient is no longer here'. The man who attains is not the man who aspires, and the goal, in relation to the two, is not the same; the bold lover, indeed, can 'never never kiss', for then he is no longer bold nor she a maid. The agitated multiform world we look out upon is a dead and ghostly world, already fixed in the mosaic of the past—a world in which Tantalus for ever stretches out his hand for the vanishing fruit, and the sword for ever impends over Damocles; for the smallest space is greater than the infinitesimal point of the present. (It is true that modern physics claims to have discovered in the atom a world where Zeno's argument does not apply—where the electrons can change place, like Scholastic angels, without passing through intervening space; but Greek thought would have found this idea as impious as numbers that have no square roots—or a god that could really suffer the pains of mortality.) In the Eleatics we have our first glimpse of the Abyss—by the very strength and passion of their denial of it—that Abyss which haunted the Middle Ages, and which the shoemaker of Seidenberg saw at the end of his last; the Parmenidean One is the crystal ball which the fiery bird held over the Deep in the fairy-tale of Grimm. The divisions of the measurable in Zeno's paradoxes have their modern equivalent in the psychological 'damp-proof courses' created by the human Will between man and man in the weird philosophic edifices of Heidegger and Sartre. The arrow, for Zeno, hung motionless in the air—*we* know that man is transfixed by the arrow. What Greek intellect could only conceive as an infinite divisibility of spaces, our modern feeling prefers to picture as the infinite intension of forces and of wills; the ancients saw the rock—*we* sense the whirlpool. Both arguments are paradoxical expressions of the incommensurability of Eternity and Time, of the Self and the Not-Self. To expound their fallacies, in the manner of the text-books of physics and psychology, is completely to miss the metaphysical point—a point which is not affected by proofs of the fact (a fairly obvious one in any case) that neither absolute Unity nor absolute Plurality can be predicated of the real world as we know it.

Heraclitus

THERE ARE many examples in history of a true definition being reached through a seeming *reductio ad absurdum*; we shall see later a case of this in the disputes of realist and nominalist, but the first and best instance is the pre-Socratic discussion about the Many and the One. When Zero argued that Motion was impossible, because a thing could not be both where it is and where it is not, it was left for Heraclitus to assert that everything in fact both is and is not, and that this paradox is the very nature of Motion—Motion which is more real than the thing moved or the mind that *thinks* it. Heraclitus is the first thinker to anticipate our modern philosophy of *Time*—the first to feel the Zenonian arrow at rest in the wound of every instant. Like such moderns as Nietzsche and Proudhon, he appears to have been (in the language of the four temperaments) a melancholic, and a 'dry' soul, more Hebrew than Greek—more of a Titan than an Olympian; for the man who sees in everything the transforming element is essentially a prophet, and experiences the fiery element of Change as it were a vulture in his own liver—

his 'character', and not outward circumstance, is his 'destiny'. The contrast between Heraclitus and the urbane materialist Democritus is proverbial and over-much quoted (for 'the Weeping Philosopher' does not well describe the bitter Ephesian); in the genial vision of the Abderitan the atoms are permanent and indestructible, like citizens whose rights are guaranteed by law. Heraclitus was in the succession of the Ionian 'naturalists', who tried each to reduce the diversity of things to a single 'element' or substratum—Thales the philosopher of Water, Anaximenes the philosopher of Air, and so in turn Heraclitus the philosopher of Fire. In this they were not—as has often been assumed—making random guesses; these 'elements' correspond very well to the three eternal ways of apprehending the world—as Being, as Not-Being, and as Becoming-and-Passing-away. The gaseous state is in fact the potentiality of things, the liquid is their material and ponderable form, while heat is their principle of growth and decomposition. The solidity of organisms is due to the liquidity contained in them, for it is by the process of *drying* that they disintegrate and pass out of separate existence; or, to put it in another way, the consciousness of organic life that sustains a thing in separateness is due to the watery element in it, which reflects and 'consolidates' it with the whole—consciousness or life which is yet a breach of that whole, and contains the fiery seed of its own disruption. Heraclitus's teacher was perhaps the Ionian Anaximander, who—in the manner of Eastern religion, though with a difference—regarded the 'immoderateness' implied in individual existence as a wrong, for which things must 'make reparation to one another' by passing away, each in its turn; it is also said that Ephesus had come within the influence of Zoroaster's fire-cult. In late-Classical and Christian philosophy, the emphasis is taken off the fiery principle of Change, not to be laid on it again until we come to the age of Hegel, Marx and Bergson—in Stoic thought it is relegated to the final conflagration of the cosmos, and in Christian theology to the state after death; for reason and morality must arrest their world in order to give laws to it, however approximate—and, in the last analysis, false—the results thus obtained. Those followers of Heraclitus who logically abjured the meaning-fixing Word, preferring to converse by signs, showed that philosophy could not continue in a straight line from this point, but had to swerve aside into an era of Abstract Reason—of reasoning first from universally-admitted premisses, and later from principles laid down by an authority recognised as credit-worthy. The process was in fact none other than the universal spiralling motion announced by Heraclitus, and compared by him to that of the screw-driver. Today we can as it were hold in one thought Newtonian Law and Einsteinian Relativity, the Word and the Meaning that flouts words, reasonable Good and irrational Creativity, Death and the Life that lives Death; we can, if we so choose, be at once absolutists and logicians with Parmenides, relativists and poets with Heraclitus. But to reach that consummation it was necessary to follow the Heraclitean 'Downward Way'—the way of the Hemlock-Cup and the Cross—to its end in the sterility and abstraction of the monasteries, as in the cold bed of Dante's Hell.

Empedocles

THIS SICILIAN was, like Heraclitus, a Time-philosopher, but of a more 'spiritual' or 'romantic' turn—a hater (that is to say) rather than a worshipper of the daemon Time. He seems to us almost more of a Christian heretic than a Classical philosopher, and a little like a popular evolutionist of the 19th Century—a century during which he was a favourite figure. In harmony with this character, he appears to have been something of a philanthropist and a 'liberal' in politics; he had moreover, if we may judge by the legend—however apocryphal—of his jumping into Etna, a taste for self-imposed martyrdom. His achievement was to marry the cyclic doctrines of the Greeks to a dualism which strikes us as un-Hellenic, to combine the doctrines of Parmenides and Heraclitus by means of an almost modern historical relativism. In the two forces of Love and Hate which alternately govern his time-epochs, we see a foreshadowing of that drama—or melodrama—which is no longer a *catharsis* but a heady morality: Love seeking its affinity, till all are One—Hate seeking the adulterous unions of the Different, till all is again a Chaos—with human (and all organic) life as a transition between these—so to speak, the Ice Age and the Heat-Death. Tennyson's Evolution 'ever striving' and Reversion 'ever dragging'. In Empedocles the mathematical idea of Eternal Recurrence acquires a mystico-scientific tinge, and merges with a yet more sensational idea (a form of what later came to be called the Ontological Argument, and which is very difficult to refute)—the idea that all the mind's fictions are facts which have occurred and will recur, from 'the brutish gods of Nile' to the monsters of H. G. Wells—the theory that the alliances of Love and Hate must result in every conceivable progeny, that the Maker and Unmaker between them must 'try everything once'. Such a notion has something in common with extreme Darwinism, and also with extreme Nominalism, for it really abolishes the concept of Species; and it is certainly surprising that no other philosopher should have thought it worth stating or examining. (We shall find an argument which, in effect, refutes it in Leibniz.) It is to be noted here that the 'One' of Empedocles is, virtually, the 'Moist' of Heraclitus—his 'Many' is the other's 'Dry'—the Many live the Death and die the Life of the One; the Sicilian philosopher's 'Love' is the Ephesian's 'Downward Way', by which Space for a while gains the upper hand over Time—the homogeneous Water over the disruptive Fire. In so far as Man distinguishes himself from Nature, the Male from the Female, or the Earth from surrounding Space, these are manifestations of 'Hate'. This suffices to show the constant interdependence of the principles, which the grandiose myth of Empedocles tended to set unduly apart; it also shows the danger of equating 'Hate' (pride or will) with the Evil or purely retrograde—a fashion which has persisted among evolutionary idealists. One may guess that the Sicilian was inclined to over-stress the principle of 'Like seeks Like' owing to that age's ignorance of electrical phenomena—the associative tendency of liquids being so much more readily observed. (He is quoted as having said, when asked why a certain dog chose to sleep always on the same tile, that the dog possessed something which was 'like to the tile'.) It is the sundering principle of 'Hate' that creates the eye, the unifier—the Eye which is also the 'I'—the same element that burns us also lights us. This idea is well symbolised by Empedocles in his theory of perception—the theory that the eye is, as it were, a lantern protected by transparent and porous plates, through which the fiery particles shoot forth and combine with similar particles outside; an idea scientifically no doubt a trifle naïve, but expressing the truth, finely stated by Goethe, that we possess sight because there is in us something that is sun-like.

Anaxagoras

WITH ANAXAGORAS the ordering and designing *Mind* first appears on the speculative horizon—that Mind which, like the sun we work by, hides from us so much more of the universe than it reveals or makes plain. He was not, however, enough of an intellectualist to please those earnest day-labourers who were to follow him, Plato and Aristotle, and he still dealt (to their disapproval) in such agents as 'air, ether and water and other eccentricities'. Thought has not yet quite 'emptied the haunted air and gnoméd mine'—Plato has not yet come to scourge the poets out of the groves of logic; but Anaxagoras has about him, unmistakably, already something of the professor. The function of Mind, in his system, was so far merely to set up a whirling Centre—the cause of all subsequent life and movement, and of the separation of the primal mass into the gaseous, the liquid and the solid. These elements, like Christianity's souls, are not altogether the 'simple substances' they appear to be; for, according to this philosopher, they are composed of particles each one of which is a compendium, in miniature, of everything in the universe. (Thus snow, he declared, was partly black—an idea which is an interesting anticipation of an important optical principle.) One is reminded of the Monadology of Leibniz, who stood to Kant in somewhat the same relation as that in which Anaxagoras was to stand to Plato; it is a rather faery-like morning world of crystal-globules. The idea had of course to wait, for its exact statement, till the concept of *relations* had replaced that of *substances*; we may accept the view that the atoms are 'seeds' without granting all that is implied in the ancient botanic theory of preformation. But the correspondence of small and great is implied in the very notion of a single Pattern. It is an idea that should particularly appeal to the introversion of our modern minds; and it also contains a suggestive hint of the relativity of size, and the fancy that there may be men like ourselves not only in the stars but—unthinkable Lilliputians—in each one of the sand-specks of the sea.

Democritus

THE MATERIALISTIC pessimism of Democritus brought him into disfavour with Athenian philosophers, but he was later to achieve a proportionate posthumous success among some of the best minds of the Roman Empire. His materialism, unlike that of his followers Epicurus and Lucretius, seems to have been carried lightly; the dance of the atoms inspired him to a cheerfulness of temper similar to that of the French Impressionists, who turned away from the apriorisms of Subject, and gave themselves up to a delighted study of Matter in all its moods. There lives indeed more truth in such materialism that in half the idealisms; as a world of Accident is more poetic than a world of Purposes which protest too much. The hopelessness of Democritus's Void is the best background for the lyric and the short tale—for the beauty of what Blake called 'the minute particulars, the mutual forgivenesses'—for whatever is small and pathetic, like an atom; it is only in works of the grand scale that its sadness becomes monotony. 'He who has never hoped can never despair' is a good motto, but scarcely for a Caesar—or a Socrates. Democritus (if not rather his master Leucippus) enjoys the dubious renown of having discovered the Atom; though his atoms were not particularly like those of modern physics. The fact, however, that his 'Atomic Theory' was the symbol for a particular feeling about the Cosmos—and not (naturally) the result of any 'impartial' laboratory-researches—entitles him to be called a most interesting philosopher. (It has unfortunately to be insisted upon again and again in our age that philosophy is not science, nor even a 'methodology' for science.) With Democritus the Mind ('*Nous*'), which entered the world-picture with Anaxagoras, again withdraws from it—saving him from the error (an error that vitiates most theological thinking) of confusing 'First' with Final Causes, and giving his theory, with its limitations, the advantages of unity and clarity. The vortexes that generate our countless worlds are due, in his system, to the collision of atoms in an emptiness—and he is the first thinker (perhaps) to conceive that there are other worlds than this in the deeps of space. Democritus is also noteworthy for having opened that now rather weary Problem of Knowledge, which we have come to regard as almost the only problem in philosophy—and therefore, naturally, as an unanswerable one—for we forget that the world of philosophy is a self-contained pattern-world, where two questions can cancel out and add up to an answer, and two doubts be equal to a faith. The solution favoured by Democritus was in fact that of the English empiricists more than 2000 years later—he distinguished the 'primary' from the 'secondary' qualities, the penny plain (so to say) from the twopenny coloured. We shall see later that Plato, and that opposite *rationalist* school deriving from him, which includes most medieval and Renaissance thinkers, adopted very nearly the contrary theory; for them it is the Ideas which are the twopenny plain, the things of sense the mere penny coloured. We may here affirm our belief that the task which remains for Western thought is to eliminate the abstraction 'Matter' without falling into solipsism, and the abstraction 'Mind' without embracing pragmatism—to make these two denials between them yield an affirmation. It is a task in which real philosophers and real mystics should find themselves at one, and where both must be content to learn from the artists, with their tremendously important concept of *Significance*. The nearest attempt at an answer yet made was that of Bishop Berkeley, though the terms of his argument are no longer fully acceptable to us. But in the systems of Plato and Democritus there is still a feeling of air around the stars and the glow-worms—the Ideas and the Atoms; the purity of the reason (as later, with the earliest Christians, the purity of the body) is not at first merely pedantry; the Democritean Void is nearer to the Great Void of Chinese philosophy than to the Abyss of the Irrational. The mild citizen of Abdera under his plane-tree, even more than the moralistic restless Plato, still represents the best ideal of the sage.

Socrates

WITH SOCRATES, philosophy deserts its contemplative isolation, the intuitive springs of its childhood, and appears—like a dry and rather 'puckish' wind—in the market-place. Himself a man of deep though perplexed faith, Socrates is the father of all doubters; he would have respected Jesus, but (one imagines) he would have been delighted with Pilate's question, and the immortal confrontation would have seemed to him merely a lost opportunity for a discussion. To the Greek or Roman rationalist, whatever could not be elucidated in words was not true—the Real was the completely Knowable—as for us today, whether we are mystics or mathematicians, truth cannot be put directly into words—the strongest runner still cannot catch up with Zeno's tortoise. Socrates was in fact a Sophist, which meant approximately a pedagogue, but he was an educator who held the modern view that to educate means to educe or elicit; his theory of 'reminiscence' (more, one fancies, a working hypothesis than a philosophical idea) seems an anticipation of the school of Dr. Jung. He was interested, enormously, in Man, but (if one can separate his thought from Plato's) very little in the Cosmos; Nature, he declared, had nothing to teach. One thinks of him as the first *Character*—a man with a restless urge, a Johnson or a Tolstoy—fascinated with the new game of dialectics as was Chesterton with paradoxes: the perfect hero for a philosopher who was also a superb novelist—a man almost as much greater than he as (in the great Reversal of all values) St. Paul was less than his Master. Strangely, in that perfection-worshipping Greek world, his very ugliness and eccentricity endear him to his acquaintances; though he has none of the unmannerliness which we have come to associate with 'character', and he reminds us a little—on the surface—of the gracious agnostic sages of China. He is instructed, as one knows, by a 'Daemon'—a Voice that gives him warnings and directions, though only of a negative character; such 'psychic' phenomena, indeed, are more common in the lives of soldiers and men of action than in those of poets and thinkers. But the Daemon of Socrates is no 'Dark God'; the turbid idea of Will is almost entirely lacking in the mathematical-minded Greeks (though it glimmers in Empedocles), and Weininger was thinking like an Oriental when he saw the twenty-four hours' meditation of Potidaea as an analogue of the Temptation. Socrates' views on art are those of the later Tolstoy—he disapproves of Aeschylus, and makes the youthful Plato burn his exercises in drama; he rates Homer lower than Aesop the fabulist, as Shaw set Bunyan above Shakespeare. Only the shadow of death makes him turn, with a certain wistfulness, to poetry. His famous 'simplicity', one feels, is more than a pleasant affectation; he was probably sincere enough when he said that Heraclitus's book 'needed a strong diver'—was, we would translate, too deep for him. His positive ideas seem to resolve themselves into two—the two dangerous half-truths of ethical rationalism and the 18th Century 'Enlightenment'—that to be truly wise (as we say, intelligent) is to be virtuous, and that to be virtuous is to be happy. The second of these propositions would tend to lead to a coarse utilitarianism, the first to moral anarchy; and in fact his accusers (one of whom, Anytus, was of a noble stamp) seem to have had some justification for seeing in him—as many have seen, not quite unjustly, in Shaw—a demoralising influence. Those who extol Socrates as a martyr for his ideas speak a language which would have been strange to him, and take away the greatest charm of the man—which was his utter lack of self-consciousness. Ever since the stupendous Tragedy of Calvary, with its cosmic implications, it has been almost impossible for European men deliberately to choose death without self-dramatisation—without 'seeing themselves in a part'. Socrates, like most Greeks, never gave a thought to posterity, and it certainly did not occur to him for one moment to regard his death as a decisive occasion in history; he considered it simply the rather bothersome result of a misunderstanding—a misunderstanding in which it would have been unmanly to seek for an accommodation. Touching immortality, one prefers to see his mind in the glorious jests of the *Apology* than in the argumentation and rhapsody put into his mouth (one fancies) by Plato in the *Phaedo*; and we read that book less for an answer to our questions than for a picture (amid our barbarism) of how civilised men could meet—and mete out—death.

Plato

A MODERN man approaches the tremendous name of Plato with very divided feelings. On the one hand we recognise him to be the greatest of philosophers—a philosopher who was also one of the greatest of all artists in prose—a writer who, we feel, could have been any sort of writer. On the other hand we detect in him something that wearies us, as it wearies us in so much of the art of Greece—a quality that to our minds is unaesthetic. The ideal Forms or Archetypes which he speaks of in the strain of a poet and a mystic are logical universals—counters from which every individual image has been erased; it comes as a slight shock to us, after reading Plato's fervent pages, to realise that his Heavenly Choir is simply a heap of abstract concepts, hypostasised as substantial souls (such concepts more especially as Temperance, Justice, the State, etc.), and that his Jacob's Ladder is in fact nothing other than the pedestrian Inductive Reason. It is hard for us to recapture the mood in which bare logical categories could seem to be objects for 'erotic' enthusiasm'; yet we have professors in universities—befoozled by words such as 'Beauty', 'Truth' and 'Harmony'—who claim that Plato told us all we need to know about the aesthetic experience. The faculty by which the Eternal Ideas, according to Plato, are delightedly apprehended is 'Knowledge'—as opposed to the mere instinctive 'Opinion' by which the Things of Time are perceived; whereas to our minds—remembering Eden—it is Knowledge, however useful, which kills, and the instinctive Intuitions—those personal Intuitions that vary from one to another of us, that come from we know not where—which alone inspire and make us alive. Real and vital Knowledge is better attained, we feel, by adding together our separate subjective impressions than by abstracting from them (by taking, so to say, their Lowest Common Denominator rather than their Highest Common Factor); and every conclusion appears to us less interesting, and less true, than the immediately-apprehended Fact. Plato's Ideas seem to us both dusty and chilly, like tomb-stones—though tomb-stones of the finest design and workmanship; and his Hellenic admiration for repose seems to have carried him to an almost Manichean yearning to be out of the body. In Plato we recognise that obsession of the Greek mind with logic and geometry—the trait which makes Greek temples and ceramics the easiest of all artefacts to imitate by machinery, and which makes us almost grateful to Time (or cunning Levantine traders) for breaking the arms or noses off Greek statuary, as if to give poor human fancy some little room for her play amidst all that too-lifeless perfection. If our modern life, our industry and social 'idealism', is blighted by standardisation— if the very word 'ideal' has come to ring hollow—we owe this in large part to Plato, who was the first to think of the 'Ideas' after the manner of moulds or stamps. But in fact our reaction against Plato is itself the result of that humanism which we learned from the great Athenians; and it is a little unfair to complain if the gift of Reason which we received from Greece has proved, in our hands, to be indeed a 'Grecian gift'. Reason, we should remember, delivered man from his agoraphobia before the jungle of impressions—even if it has ended by substituting for it that claustrophobia which, in modern minds, so often verges dangerously on solipsism; and only those artists have the right to be 'impressionists' who have first gone to school with the Greeks. In all things not human, the logical idea concurs, nearly enough, with the aesthetic idea—the universal with the individuality; the particular nature and habit of (say) the lion is almost as well discovered by taking an average of all actual lions as by the more direct vision of the poet, who sees the 'leonine-ness' in each specimen of that species. The discovery of *classes* has made the masterpieces of Nature for the first time steadily legible and decipherable, instead of uncertainly and fitfully so—long as humanity had to wait for that true and best Platonist, the humble Wordsworthianly-religious natural scientist of the Romantic Era. And if Man were just another classifiable species—merely a rational animal or an embodied spirit—it would be right to say with the Hellenistic metaphysicians that Jesus was the Perfect or Divine Man; because, of those virtues which men should have in common (the *moral* virtues namely), he possessed, of men known to us, perhaps the largest measure. That language is unsatisfying to us today, because—with increase of our historical age—we have learned that every individual man is, inasmuch as he is a *self*, essentially a separate species, and that we can no more truly compare man with man than we can give one law to the lion and the ox. The belief in the personal 'Soul' has been the solvent of all the systems and creeds that were set up to shelter its beginnings. The essential Form of Socrates is not Man or the Wise Man, but the *character*, the living 'I', of Socrates; and the artist in Plato knew it well, though the thinker would hardly even have understood so foreign a notion. The essential Form of the State or 'Justice' is not Plato's pedantic *Republic*, or any other Utopia; it is, in their turn, each of the many possible patterns of harmonious social relationship. And in fact the best example of the Platonic fallacy can be seen in the vulgarest use of the adjective; the Greeks tried to make love itself intellectual, an education for the philosopher-citizen—and therefore to concentrate it on that sex which better reflects the Idea and is less assimilated to Nature. It is what makes the Socratic dialogues a trifle tedious and priggish compared with some conversation-parties of the Renaissance—though bathed, perhaps, in a kindlier, cooler, atmosphere. And the question of the Erotic reminds us that we are forgetting something— something that gives its peculiar clarity and (paradox though it may sound) *innocence* to Plato's world. For the human person is not only in himself a distinct species, he is condemned to unite with another person, also specifically as well as sexually distinct— a union which his metaphysical essence feels as derogatory, and which is the source of all those subconscious 'Hate'-feelings that strengthen the dark current of the Will. This necessity, the Greeks, by a transposition of the whole 'spiritual' part of sex, sought to evade, and consequently their souls, if adolescent and odd, seem to us singularly fresh and limpid. And yet we sense in Plato (as, of course, even more in the great tragedians) the hint of a dissatisfaction, a question that will not be repressed—breaking, very movingly, through his perfect prose. Why is the world so much nearer to the Idea of the Beautiful than to the Idea of the Good? Why does man's lack of 'wisdom' constitute such a rift in the total harmony? Why is Eros, in spite of everything, so disturbing to the soul's calm? Why is life, in fact, so sad that it would seem better never to have been born? Christianity's reply to that inquiry was Original Sin. We would phrase it, more generally, that man— and he alone—is tragically endowed with Originality.

Protagoras

PLATO'S DISPUTES with the Sophists seem to us to run closely parallel to the later controversies of Pascal with the Jesuits. Both occurred during a time of perplexity, when reason was undermining ancient standards; and the Sophists, like the Jesuits, believed—not always from unworthy motives—in making concessions to the Zeitgeist. But neither Plato's 'Idea of the Good' nor Pascal's Jansenistic God could be (nor, perhaps, were) expected to make much of an appeal to ordinary men. Protagoras's saying that 'Man is the measure' we take to mean that man—as a reasonable creature—will always judge every matter chiefly with reference to his desires and his immediate perceptions, and it is foolish to expect anything else. That, at least, seems more sensible than the Socratic doctrine that Reason will lead man to the Good and the True; the mere Reason cannot give any motive for just dealing or even for candid reasoning. Whether Protagoras was merely making a 'constatation', or whether he meant to advocate a sort of Pragmatism, it is at this date impossible to determine. There is also, of course, a profounder meaning of the famous aphorism—namely that man is the microcosm, and he has only to look within himself and search his heart for him to understand everything in heaven and earth. But this does not appear to have been what Protagoras had in mind.

Aristotle

PLATO HAD praised the Reason, but there is little of its dry light in his work; with him and Socrates logic is still 'dialectic'—a conversation. Aristotle is the first pure rationalist, and therefore—in temper—a dogmatist; for he who has found a rule for the discovery of truth has no need to leave his college or his cloister—if he is not, as was Plato, a devotee of beauty nor, as was Socrates, of goodness. Truth, like the Aristotelian Absolute, is self-sufficing. In the mechanism of the syllogism Aristotle perfected that very useful sort of slot-machine from which the satisfying conclusion can always be extracted upon dropping into it the coin of a minor premiss—for the major premiss, like a spring, is already in place. He was, however, enough of a Platonist to be often a poet *malgré lui*; God, he said, moves the world as the beloved object moves the lover—a God who, however, does not Himself love. Plato had spoken similarly—not however so much of the world, but rather of the soul of the philosopher—not so much of God but of the Ideas. For Plato, God (or 'the Demiurge') creates the world out of the formless Matter by contemplating the impassive Archetypes, as a sculptor works from his models. For Aristotle, on the other hand, God is Himself an inert magnetic x, merging—one cannot but feel—with the inexistent matrix at the other end of the scale, as 'Matter' merges with 'Energy 'in modern physics; the poles of Actuality and Potentiality, between which our life circles, tend to converge like North and South when pressed backward in thought to the Antipodes. It seems strange that the Greeks, so much of whose physics was vitiated by their prejudice in favour of the Circle, made little use of the idea in their metaphysics, where it really does apply (since the idea of Eternity neighbours the idea of Death.) Philosophy had to wait till Hegel for any realisation of the truth that the mind's extremes meet—whenever it is forgotten that their existence is merely logical. Aristotle is the first consistent monotheist among Greek thinkers—he substitutes the logical Absolute for Plato's half-divinised Ideas; and, like all monotheists, he at once creates a dualism—one Absolute calls up another—Evil, from being a form of Good, will before long become the very Evil. Into the house which Aristotle carefully swept of Plato's ideal furniture were soon to enter the legions of Gnostic and neo-Platonic devils and angels. It is somewhat in the same way that Protestantism and the 18th Century Deism, in stripping Christianity of saint and miracle, produced a vacuum which was soon to be filled by the demons of the secular-messianic ideologies; the guillotine, one might say—by a somewhat violent metaphor—grew out of the 'razor' of the rationalising Occam. But there is a more subtle reason why monotheism—for good and evil—tends to pass into a sort of Manichean demonism or titanism; it causes an immense potentiation of the *Will*—that Will which is barely conscious of itself in the classical Greek, as later in the Mediterranean Catholic, life and thought. Is it perhaps more than a symbol that Aristotle was the teacher of Alexander, or that Frederick owed his mental formation to the Deists? Having said this, we should add that Aristotle's immanent Forms are much nearer to our present way of thinking and feeling—even to our aesthetic feeling—than are Plato's museum-case transcendent

Forms; they are in fact related to them somewhat as are Hegel's conceptual forms to those of Kant. Moreover, they are partly conceived in the modern fashion as *relations*; that which is form in one reference is potentiality in another. We believe (it may be said in passing) that his categories of Actuality and Potentiality also provide the real answer to the Problem of Knowledge: the perceiving Mind—like a sun—draws this world of Forms out of the seed of 'Matter', and the eye of a God—or of the ideal artistic contemplator—would see the spatio-temporal picture simply in terms of Form. Again, Aristotle distinguishes, at least as a matter of grammar and logic, between the universal and the essentially non-logical notion of the individual (as e.g. between *a* lion and *the* lion)—those two ideas which Plato failed to distinguish; though, like all Greeks, he regards the universal—and the reason which apprehends it—as the divine part. This of course is to deal only with a small part of Aristotle's immense achievement, but his thought is not—like Plato's—a closely-interlocked unity; it might almost have been, as in part it no doubt was, the work of a group of encyclopedists. Though we have called his metaphysic 'Protestant', he is nevertheless Catholic—the fit teacher of the later Middle Ages—in his realistic treatment of politics and morals, and his wise criticisms of Plato's enthusiastic utopianism. He is excellent in his demonstration that monarchy is the best, tyranny the worst, of governments—democracy being somewhere in between. The *Nicomachean Ethics*, with their sober ideal of personal dignity, are at least a refreshing antidote to a secularised and deliquescent 'Christianity' ('service before self', the ideals of the Rotarian, etc.)—and are accordingly sneered at by all popular writers on philosophy. His aesthetics, though small in compass, form almost the only *apparatus criticus* existing in Europe till the present century, and contrast happily with Plato's almost pitiable deliverances on the subject. It should be observed that by *mimesis* Aristotle did not mean mere imitation but rather reflection in a mind, and that his *catharsis* is not so much the crude idea of a purgation as a resolution of discordancy—ideas upon which, indeed, modern criticism can elaborate but can hardly improve. The simple meaning of Aristotle's terms—which has been obfuscated by whole libraries of exegesis—should be perfectly clear from his use of them primarily in regard to *music*. It was Aristotle, and not Oscar Wilde, who said in his notes on the drama: 'There is no reason why *some* events that have actually happened should not conform to the law of the probable and possible'. In a word, there is much of Aristotle which we are in a better position to appreciate today than were our ancestors in the age of Scholasticism, when his authority was sacrosanct—or in the age of Romanticism when it was flouted. It is not unamusing that this least romantic among the ancient philosophers should have been turned into a folk-hero—he is known to the Irish peasantry as Harry Stotle, a vagrant and rascally tinsmith. Alas, poor Stagirite!

Stoics

IT IS HARD for a modern man to be altogether fair to Stoicism, the great pre-Christian ethical system of the ancient world; for Stoicism may be called a religion of virtue for virtue's sake. Virtue for the sake of being virtuous is a depressing doctrine, and the Stoics were, generally speaking, depressed and depressing people. They have bequeathed to us a formidable legacy of platitude, and it is their leaden touch (more than any Christian influence) that stirs the modern youth to impatience in the literature of the last four centuries; it is certainly deplorable, for instance, that Shakespeare owed whatever conscious philosophy he possessed to such a mediocre sage as Seneca. We are apt to forget that Stoicism fulfilled an important function in separating the ethical idea from custom and the will of rulers; just as the modern movement called 'art for art's sake' has separated the aesthetic idea from morals and social utility. The Stoics—and, it may be, the modern aesthetes also—are justified as the half-conscious forerunners of a new kind of man. It is easy to criticise the moral philosophy of the Stoics; their ethic was in many respects admirable, but it was to a large extent nullified in practice by their peculiar conception of 'detachment'—a detachment which had nothing of the contemplative attitude to the mystery and the tragedy of existence. The just man, they held, was unaffected by any misfortune that might befall him—he could be happy even in an engine of torture; whereas the unjust man was not *really* happy even on a throne. It is possible that this was, at the time, a necessary way of affirming moral subjectivity—of expressing the fact that the self-denials of virtue can have their compensations from a subjective point of view; but it is equally obvious that if the doctrine, as stated, were even approximately true there would be no problem of Evil. Its practical effect was, too often, to set the 'just man' prosing without end about 'justice' instead of being, actually, just. The only virtue which Stoicism certainly promoted was the doubtless basic one of self-control; but the Stoic really thought it a worse fault to be sensible of his own sufferings than to be insensitive to the—perhaps greater—sufferings of others. Such insensitiveness was, in fact, not far removed from a virtue, though the Stoics did not always draw this conclusion explicitly. Stoicism was not necessarily, as Pascal called it, a doctrine of 'diabolical pride', for firmness under misfortune can be noble; but at least it encouraged an exaggerated self-consciousness which to us is very distasteful. The Stoic 'philosopher', assisting at the whipping of one of his slaves while he expatiated on his complete freedom from the weakness of anger—interrupting himself only to order that the whipping should by no means be relaxed while he held forth—is an unenticing picture; but we may concede that in seeking to justify himself before the slave he was implying that human equality which was a (theoretical) Stoic tenet. The emperor Marcus Aurelius was able to quote with respect the slave Epictetus; but that was as far as he went in the direction of an enlightened humanitarianism. Plato's dream of the Philosopher-King was realised beyond his own dreams—and nothing was changed. It was the total failure of the Socratic Reason; the world was hungry, not for Wisdom, but for the Folly of Love. On the speculative side, Stoicism was a deterministic pantheism, rather resembling (with its two 'modes' of active thought and passive matter) the later pantheism of Spinoza; such pantheism can be near to mysticism, but Christians—from Augustine to Kierkegaard—have always tended to see in it 'diabolical pride', since it understresses the sense of sin and separation from God. The Stoic God was not Aristotle's Unmoved Mover but more like what modern vitalists call the Life-Force—identified in the pre-Socratic manner with the cyclic motion of the 'ether' (called sometimes air, sometimes fire) of which the elements are made. But the lesser gods of polytheism were allowed their place—whether from broad-mindedness or expediency—as in the somewhat similar system of Buddhism. It has often been observed that those thinkers who talk most about Virtue believe the least in Freewill; but the contradiction is only a seeming one, for a Will that is propelled into action, whether good or bad, is not free. A perfectly free Will would be in the situation of Buridan's Ass, immobilised between the good and the evil motive as the famous donkey starved between the two bundles of hay; this is in fact the position of the true contemplator, who is freed from the cause-and-effect chain, if only in the breathless instant of contemplation. In the world of action we may say (according to taste) that he is freest who is drawn on by the sole motive of the Good (or, as ethical philosophers generally fail to observe, the Bad)—or, alternatively, he who obeys whatever motive presents itself, at the moment, with the greater force. The actions of the first have the larger element of rational Choice, those of the second are the most dictated by impulsive Whim. Stoics and Christians were inclined to identify 'Freewill' with the first sort of determination, we today more usually see our 'Freedom' in the second; but both are in fact 'determined'.

Epicureans

EPICUREANISM HAS the advantage over Stoicism of having been founded by a considerably philosopher, who was also something of a saint, and in having been celebrated by a great poet, who

was in addition almost a prophet. It had, however, less of a reputation in the ancient world than Stoicism, and it has come to be thought of—very unjustly—as a doctrine of sensual indulgence. For Epicureanism was too civilised, too disabused, a creed for a world which was soon to become an arena for the mighty clashing figures of Emperors and Churchmen. The Epicurean in fact believed, as every realistic and consistent rationalist must believe, that 'the struggle nought availeth, the labour and the wounds are vain'; he sought for a tranquility in escape and fastidious seclusion, in place of the rather impossible Stoical 'apathy' in action; the Garden of Epicurus brings to our minds the *jardin* of Voltaire's famous maxim. In their attack upon religion, Epicurus and Lucretius—like many modern sceptics—were actuated by philanthropy as well as conviction, a philanthropy which seems to us almost Christian in tone; they wished to deliver mankind from the fear of death and Hades. It is, however, only tired, too-reasonable, people who can fancy that the fear of death springs, in any large degree, from the fear of continued suffering—gloomy though most eschatologies have undoubtedly been; it is normally, for the greater part, no more than the obverse of the love of life, and the demons of the underworld are symbols for the woes of depravity or dissolution. In its ethic, though not in its cosmology, Epicureanism has much affinity with Buddhism, as there is a certain similarity between Epicurus and Gautama; both were gentle, sad, sages preaching a rational asceticism, a sort of spiritual hygiene. The true Epicurean would follow the counsel of Swift:
> Drink little at a time,
> Put water in your wine,
> Miss your glass when you can,
> Go out the first man.

One might feel inclined to protest that 'It's a poor heart which never rejoices', but Epicureanism, one remembers, had also an attractive positive side. This is shown, in the verse of Lucretius, by a clean love of non-human nature, stripped of the trappings of the pathetic fallacy, and, in the life of Epicurus, by the cult of friendship—friendship in which women and slaves were, for the first time in antiquity, invited to share. When one searches for notable examples of the spiritual life, one dwells perhaps with less pleasure on preachers, martyrs and militant orders (saving only very few exceptions) than on groups which have set a high value on friendship, without needing either the normal human motive of conviviality nor the base one of mutual advancement—groups such as the first Quakers, the early Christians, the Epicureans, the Pythagoreans. Epicurus, moreover, professed a quasi-aesthetic non-utilitarian devotion to the gods—gods thought of as ideal types, somewhat like Plato's Forms, dwelling in a state of calm Epicurean blessedness, in a world far removed from 'the sphere of our sorrow'. In physics, where the Stoics looked back—mainly —to Heraclitus, the Epicureans closely followed Democritus; but with an important difference, which suffices to establish Epicurus as an original thinker. The atoms, which for Democritus fell 'downwards' in the Void like a rain, are endowed by Epicurus with a power—ever so slight—of spontaneous 'declination'. In this way, as he thought, he both answered Aristotle's objection (that the falling atoms of Democritus could never make contact) and rescued human freedom—freedom which in all the early thought of the world, and especially Greek thought, is wholly subject to the Fates; for the Soul, according to Epicurus, though material and mortal, was 'Free'—being composed of atoms of the finest and most volatile kind. The generation which has discovered Quantum Theory is less likely to laugh at this idea than were the scientists of the past. Whatever exactly is meant by Heisenberg's 'principle of Indeterminacy'—or however it may be modified by the course of research—it is at least clear that the norms of the atomic world are very different from those of the world of 'commonsense'. This would seem to confirm the natural-enough belief—first asserted by Epicurus—that the incalculable and unpredictable complexity of human persons (commonly, though not quite accurately, called 'Freewill') corresponds to an incalculable complexity in the inmost nature of 'matter' itself.

Philo & Apollonius

WITH THE syncretist Philo and the neo-Pythagorean Apollonius, the streams of Hellenism and Hebraism, of philosophy and theology, for the first time converge; we get our first hints of the great Synthesis which to so many minds—and by no means mediocre ones only—has seemed a completely final and satisfying Explanation of Things. That Synthesis, like the Hindu Trinity, was to be in turn a Destroyer, a Preserver and a Creator for mankind. It acted in part as a solvent of the old civilisation (already doomed, certainly, from other causes), but it preserved the best of that civilisation's thought under the guise—as we must regard them—of symbols and allegories, and out of this salvage it created a new world, a truly 'brave new world'—the Europe we know or until lately knew. In Philo we see the allegorising process commencing—Greek philosophy becomes a gloss upon the Pentateuch, the Platonic Forms are transformed into generative Forces, Thoughts or uttered Words of a Thinker—the operative term of the new era will be the *Logos*. For the Jews, God had always been a Creator *de toutes pièces*, as for the Platonic philosophy He was what the 18th Century called a 'Designer'; the creation of the world had been a sheer Miracle—the first of the many miracles by which He marked the stages of His mysterious Way. It was the Divine Will rather than the Divine Reason which the Jewish Scriptures had stressed, and belief in which had given the race its strange toughness in adversity; Job accepts his misfortunes, not—like a Stoic—from 'Reason', but from a sense of the impotence of Reason. Now, Reason and Will are to merge in the essentially human and allegorical notion of the Word—the *Name* which goes with the Person, and *is* the Person. Everything now is personalised—the mathematical Greek concepts will soon re-appear as Christian and neo-Platonist Powers and Principalities. For the idea of Personality (that scandal to the mere thinker) had been missed or evaded by the great Greeks—we have seen how the Pythagorean mathematicians dreaded the thought of the Incommensurable. The old philosophy was a preserve for intellectuals; there was nothing to feed the hearts of common men—more particularly the enormous, greatly-suffering, slave-population—except the old legends of polytheism, fallen more and more into discredit and disrepute. Now Judea, with its monotheistic tradition and Messianic promise, had to supply what Athens could not give. Humanity resembled a boy who—tired both of abstract lessons and his nursery-tales, and becoming conscious of his developing Ego—looks around him for a Model, an older boy or favourite master whom he may serve with a shy and dog-like devotion; and the need, we must think, created the God-Man. The text-books of philosophy which over-leap the fifteen centuries between Plotinus and Descartes (inserting maybe one brief chapter on Scholasticism) show a professorish misunderstanding of the meaning of Dogma—the symbolic statement that veils but also reveals; a professorish trust, moreover, in the power of logical analysis to define the non-logical element in existence. At this point in our story Philosophy, dazzled by the brilliance of the Grecian day, re-descended into Plato's Cavern and spoke to the prisoners—in the language of the shadows—of the glories it had seen. For the few partially-enlightened thinkers, it was as if a night had fallen on the earth. For the many gropers in darkness, it was as if they beheld a great light.

Clement of Alexandria

FOR ANYONE with 'a relish of philosophical things', there can have been few more exciting places to live in at any time than Alexandria in the first centuries of the Christian Era. There life seems to have been a perpetual Pentecost, in which the tidings of the Incarnation—like a furious wind—ran through the innumerable Greek schools and Syrian cults; for to all of them it was a 'scandal' to be explained, a 'paradox' to be assimilated. A faint parallel can be seen in the shock caused to the intellect of modern Europe by the rediscovery of Evil—not as a mere accident of maladjustment in human life, but almost as what Christianity calls it, 'the Spirit of this World'; the divers 'Existential' schools of today—with their incantatory language—seem like a reflexion of the 'Gnostic' sects of that age. The Gnostics, we should say, were in the right in the distinction they drew between philosophy and the popular theology; but they were wrong (as the school of historical relativism might put it) in the context of the mental habits and language which they shared with their contemporaries— a falsity which forced them to be much more 'popular' (in the sense of a vulgar mystagogy) than the Churchmen whom they affected to despise. The best minds of the time, in fact, were to be found in the Catholic body—not among these now forgotten representatives of a debased intellectualism. It must be said on the other hand that it was possible then, as for good and for ill it has scarcely been possible since the Nicene formulation (save perhaps during the Early Renaissance) for men of free speculative temper to remain in communion with the Church. Such a venerated doctor as the gentle Clement of Alexandria, for instance, at almost any other period in our era would have found himself and his works condemned or burnt, for his heart was really in the Renaissance dream of a Marriage of Athens and Jerusalem, and he is in many ways nearer in spirit to Plato and Plotinus than to St. Paul and Tertullian. His God the Father is the philosopher's Absolute— the 'non-existent God' or 'Eternal Silence' of Gnostic thought, who only attains to consciousness in the person of the Son; Christ is 'the New Orpheus', and the Pauline doctrine of the Atonement barely alluded to. But Clement's perfect Christian (whom he calls the *true* Gnostic) exhibits the Stoic apathy rather than the neo-Platonic—and later Christian—ecstasy; he eats, drinks and procreates (for Clement sets the married state above the single) as nearly as possible without pleasure, just as the Arjuna of the *Bhagavad Gita* was commanded to fight and kill, but without enthusiasm. 'The true Gnostic' he says—in words unsuggestive of Christianity—'is the really perfect man and friend of God, and is placed in the rank of son.' Christian humility, we see, is not the note of Alexandrianism; and we read likewise that the possessor of knowledge (gnosis) has risen beyond faith, fear and hope. In this connection Clement has two striking phrases—in which, however, the later Christianity would have seen blasphemous Antinomianism: 'God became Man in order that men might become Gods', and 'the true Gnostic has no virtue, because he *is* virtue'. For the rest, Clement can still be read with pleasure even by the untheologically-minded; his discourses are veritable storehouses of quotation and curious lore, and often remind us by their style of the great essayists of the 17th Century. His must be the only reference to the Buddha in the literature of Europe until modern times; and he drops easily into the cult-language of the Eleusinian mysteries. We are charmed when he warns us against sleeping in carved bedsteads, because such harbour reptiles, or wearing the hair too thick lest it should injure the brain; or when he compares wealth with a serpent which, unless caught and held with caution, will double back and bite the hand. 'Man' he says 'is a laughing animal'—and again (too optimistically) 'Man is a creature of peace'. Clement is Plato's Attic sun dwindled to a candle by a cot—a happy bird of the hedgerows ministering, half-ignorant, to an alien fledgling cuckoo.

Tertullian

TERTULLIAN—the first great literary genius of Latin Christianity—has been compared to St. Paul: an inverted, as Paul was a converted, persecutor; little of a Christian, for those to whom Christianity means St. Francis but not St. Dominic. In fact, however, without such uncomfortable zealots as Paul and Tertullian, the Christian Church would probably have left as little trace on the coming centuries as any obscure Gnostic sect. As God had humbled Himself by becoming human, man (it may be said) had now to humble himself by becoming, in the best as well as the worst sense, primitive—hot-blooded but tractable, sometimes as a mindless animal, sometimes as a holy child. From Tertullian's writings it is clear that in early life he had been a patron of the amphitheatres, and was won over by the spectacle of Christian fortitude more than by an intellectual process. 'Martyrdom proves nothing', we are inclined to say; but to speak so is to misconceive the whole purpose and intention of the martyrs. The Early Christians did not sacrifice their lives to prove any abstract proposition or objective truth; rather they wished to show that there was a power in them stronger than the power of the Caesars, the power namely of the dedicated will and of detachment from the life of sense—in the new, mysterious but powerful language invented by St. Paul, 'Not them but Christ in them'. Soldiers, indeed, had died in all times for their country, or their city; a Regulus could return to his captors to be tortured; the idea of loyalty was familiar enough to the dutiful Roman spirit. Now Romans and Romanised barbarians were to prove their loyalty to an invisible city—to proclaim a super-sensual happiness which made the grossest pains of sense to seem as nothing. Suffering was to be no longer an accident in the Cosmos, a bitter slavery, a cruel jest; God Himself, by taking on Himself the sorrowful human condition, had infused suffering with new meaning. Men could become God-like, not—as the ancient and modern sages have thought—through knowledge, but rather through faith unto death, faith which was a homage paid by the instincts and not a mere mental persuasion; 'Man's first disobedience', through which came the Mind's good and evil, could be expiated by the Heart's obedience to the sole good—like a sin of the body repaired by the sacrament of marriage. This was the revolution which was 'absurd', 'impossible', and yet true: true, indeed, by its very absurdity—for how could that other world speak to this one except through the medium of Paradox and Miracle? Tertullian—turbulent, unregenerate indeed, but a fighter and a poet in grain—rose superbly to the challenge. There is in him also an ominous hint of a real morbid streak in Christendom—that climate of Early Christianity which Nietzsche compared to a Russian novel—the sense that the holy Murder of Calvary has dipped all our hands in blood, as every martyrdom makes of the beneficiaries partners in its guilt. 'Have you a mind for blood?' he says, 'You have the blood of Christ'. All this side of him is familiar to us from the urbane disgust of Gibbon. But let us not carp; let us abandon ourselves to the pleasure of saying the words—the greatest ever wrung from a mind tortured by insoluble contradictions—words which so strangely bring the age of the Martyrs down to the age which has discovered Kierkegaard: 'The Son of God was crucified, I am *not* ashamed of it because men must needs be ashamed of it; and the Son of God died, it is utterly credible because it is absurd; and He was buried and rose again, it is certain because it is impossible'.

Origen

ORIGEN WAS a greater intellect than his master Clement, though he was—even more than Clement—what the church of Marx calls a 'deviationist'. He is interesting for his share in the discussion which was to culminate in that highest achievement of religious dogmatics, the so-called Athanasian Creed. Every great philosophy has in fact been a variation on that central theme—precisely of the Theme, the Variation and the Development—of the Absolute, the Relative, and that mutual Correspondence which makes of the Absolute itself, in a sense, Relatedness; each has been an attempt to state, whether imaginatively or abstractly, that contradiction at the heart of things which is yet mysteriously an identity —the formula whereby the One resolves and is resolved into the Many, by means of which the 'monistic' key can revolve in the 'pluralistic' lock. In Plato and the Pythagoreans the distinction between the Idea and the Thing, and the third, more shadowy, notion of a Spirit or 'Life-Force' conjoining them—as it were the non-existent Point, the Circumference and the outgoing Radius—is already clearly discernible; but the Greeks had unduly depreciated the real in favour of the ideal and essential. The Incarnation—and the whole of the Early Christian preoccupation with the question of *Substance*—was an attempt to raise the 2nd Person of the Triad to his proper dignity, to integrate the real and human in the divine. That preoccupation it has been the custom to regard as one of the showpieces of human imbecility; but we may understand it if we realise how very shocking to the thought of antiquity was the belief in the 'taking on of the Flesh'. Our minds, schooled by Christianity, are apt to take an optimistic or romantic (indeed over-romantic) view of corporeal life, maternity and sex, where the ancients felt nothing but a deep abjection. Christianity is wrongly credited with inventing the shame of the body, because it brought men the promise of an emancipation from its toils; the promise had indeed a tendency to be visionary or exaggerated, like that of the utopian socialist who dreams of a 'Leisure State', but the socialist intellectual has not *invented* a revulsion from labour's servitude unfelt by the natural man—only those persons who, thanks to Christianity or civilisation, have never felt the pitiableness of the human condition could fall into either error. Sex may have its glory and labour its dignity, but only through that 'Descent' of the 3rd member of the Trinity pointed to by the 4th Evangelist, an infusion which is still perhaps no more than humanity's Hope. That Hope, for the contemporaries of St. John, had to be explained—if it was not to be, on idealist or rationalist theories, explained away—by the dogmas of the Incarnation and miraculous Virgin-birth: agony and sweat *could*, in some sense, be divine—conception *could*, in some sort, be pure —the demonish *Sophia* of the Gnostics could be replaced by the blessed Mary. Origen, one of the first great explainers, is important by his stressing of the 'Co-Eternity of the Son'—'*There is not when He was not*'—we should interpret, the necessity for Love to have an Object, even before that Object palpably *exists*; as also for the paradox, maintained by him, of the Son's *voluntary* Subordination—the single Will taking alternately the active and the passive part—an analogy with human relationships which saves distinction from ending in polytheistic anarchy. By a similar taste for metaphysical symmetry, he 'lapsed' into the heresies of the soul's pre-existence and the ultimate salvation of the damned—ideas which (like the Eastern reincarnation) were felt, no doubt rightly, to lessen the urgency of the Christian spiritual appeal. For what remains, Origen is notable for his performances in the allegorical interpretation of Scripture—those 'meanings at four levels' with which, as a method, we are rather wearisomely familiar in Dante, but which were to illustrate (once more) the Christian idea of a Divine Complexity. His application of it to the Song of Songs set a precedent for countless works of erotic mystification, but a similar line of thought (in Ignatius) produced the deeply-suggestive exclamation 'My Eros is crucified'. In his great controversy with Celsus he reveals a belief in the magical efficacy of names for defeating the demons—that lower or superstitious side of religion which all doctrines of the saving grace of dogmas or ceremonials in fact imply. But in general he is a freer and more civilised mind than most of his successors, though without Augustine's poignancy and power.

Plotinus

THE GREATEST of the Alexandrians was no Christian but the neo-Platonist Plotinus—one of the greatest, indeed, of men who have lived: great, perhaps, less in his achievement, wonderful though it is, than in his symbolic significance. In him Greek thought, like an aged Moses, was given sight of the Promised Land which it could never enter and possess—for the schools of Plato and Pythagoras, sunk in magic and theurgy, had become content to 'strike the rock', and out of them could proceed no new word for humanity; after him the dogmatic Aarons had to take over the command from the sages. But in Plotinus the ancient Wisdom almost caught fire from the young altars of Faith. Plotinus is the first and perhaps the most perfect of that high and rare order of philosophers, the speculative mystics—those thinkers who are able to combine a rapture which is fundamentally aesthetic with logical analysis. The intuition and the reason have at all times paired together as ill as the spirit and the flesh, and the mystics have tended to despise abstract thought as much as the philosophers have been prone to distrust enthusiasm; the poetical fervour of Plato was not (as we have indicated) a truly mystical one, any more than the reasonings of the monks had anything to do with speculation. The consequences of that divorce we see in the divided modern 'psyche'. Today the 'mystic' has come to mean almost exclusively—in the Catholic world—the ecstatic Counter-Reformation saint, or on the other hand—outside the Churches—the Indian Yogi, neither of whom can properly be called a philosopher; while, in the half-secularised but still fermenting world of Protestantism, mysticism has been absorbed—not helpfully—into various philosophic schools, those of the idealism of Hegel or the subjectivism of Kierkegaard. The rationalist concentrates on the text 'I am the Light of the World', the existentialist glosses on that other text 'My God, my God, why hast Thou forsaken me?' The one stresses the self-sufficiency of the brain, the other the sense of deficiency of the heart, and between them the mystic's joy—the Plotinian 'flight of the alone to the Alone'—altogether escapes. Following Kant—and Descartes and Plato and all—we have over-prized the *visual* (which is as much as to say the merely *verbal*) element in thought, as electricity has abolished our twilights; the dim half-animal sense of mental *touch*, the 'sensual logic' of the primitive, is found only in such 'sports' as William Blake and D. H. Lawrence—even the mystic's goal of 'the One' has come to suggest that depressing or dangerous idea, the mathematical Infinite. It is our belief that philosophy, at present living among the husks of pragmatism and logical positivism, must be brought back to mysticism, its true home and spouse; and when that should happen Plotinus will perhaps be recognised as the greatest saint in its calendar. In the narrower sense, Plotinus is interesting for his theory of the Trinity—conceived not as a transcendence merely, but as the very structure of reality; and we find a hint of a later controversy in the two aspects of the 3rd hypostasis. He is the first philosopher to state clearly the Berkeleian principle that Matter is illusory, the Kantian principle that Space —its creator—is a subjective form of the mind, the Hegelian principle that thought and reality are one; he even anticipates Descartes (not quite consistently with these assertions) in confronting the problem of 'interaction'. For him it is the Mind that creates the ideas of things by contemplating the One, not—as with Plato—the Demiurge that creates the World by contemplating the

Ideas; but in both of them the lower hypostasis, at each level, reflects the higher—a 'reflexion' which is also an act of mental *reflection*. Only that for Plotinus the One is (in the language of later mystics) a 'Hiddenness', at the centre of soul and mind, which can be touched only at the rarest intervals—whereas for Plato the 'Idea of the Good' is the philosopher-statesman's broad daylight. He argues, profoundly, that the Beautiful is second to the Good because its apprehension is fleeting and the aspiration after it painful; on his principles he should rather, for these reasons, have placed it first. Plotinus is like Plato in having an inadequate sense of Evil (that thorn in the side of the Christians and the Gnostics), but he is unlike him—a child of the new, ever-darkening, era—in having no real hope for the world. Much of his work affects us as tedious by the usual Stoical, unconvincing, demonstrations that the wise man can be happy in all circumstances—which he combines, illogically enough, with the equally unconvincing, easy-optimistic, doctrine of Karma. But Plotinus—a mystic in an age of superstition—has nothing about him of the charlatan, though this cannot be said of most of the 'neo-Platonists'; in regard to astrology he holds the view—consonant with his sense of universal 'sympathy'—that the stars repeat and reflect, but do not determine, our life-patterns. Again unlike his Greek teachers, and agreeing with the Christians, he maintains that individuals are specifically distinct—that each person has his own 'ideal form'; as city-state and empire had declined, the notion of the individual had grown. The Incarnation, however, was necessarily repugnant to his idealities; in his cosmic joys, as in Wordsworth's, there is something elderly, world-weary, and a little forced; the 'dialectic' of the Ideas in history and society he did not, like Augustine, attempt to explore; so that his system remains, after all, a Classic temple—perfect but closed upon itself.

Augustine

TO PASS FROM Plotinus to Augustine is like leaving a cool though glowing garden to enter a hothouse. Augustine is the dialectician of the Heart—a heart sufficiently complex for us to recognise in it the familiar modern Mother-Mistress 'split'; whether or no those celebrated *Confessions* of his really 'make the reader envy his transgressions', we certainly feel our love excited for so tremendous a lover—a lover whom only an Infinite Love could, finally, appease. That thirst for the invisible Source and Principle of Love—only capable of being loved, and therefore in a manner known, by Love's very nature, if we think of It as a Person—is the great youth's-romance of our race; and that it is by no means so 'dated' as a too schematic or snobbish historicism would maintain, we see today in the impressive literature of the school of Brunner and Barth. Much of Augustine's writing belongs properly to religious devotionalism rather than philosophy, and one shrinks from approaching with the tools of analysis so very human and personal an emotion as that of the Christian saint. Here is not the aesthetic exaltation of Plotinus, or even of Dante, but something much more intimate. We are at times even conscious of an embarrassment in reading—for Augustine's penitences, self-abasements and self-deceptions might nauseate us in a less fiery and tormented soul, as they so often do in Rousseau. But Augustine of course (herein alone resembling his imitator) wishes us to be the witnesses and sharers of his shames; the saints, as opposed to the true mystics, are social—even when they are hermits. Christianity, which brought the sense of sin, brought also —as its rather unlovely by-product—the need for confession: a need which yet is the root of most modern literature, and has given men that self-knowledge which the extraverted Greeks had dreamed of but could not achieve. Augustine is the true type of the saint, who suffers and overcomes great 'temptations'—as distinguished from the rarer, sweeter, character of the mystic, to whom all things are pure; but without the first we could scarcely have the second. Moreover that experience of the Abyss is also a part of the human mind; Augustine identifies it, acutely, with pure irrational self-Will—his boyhood's prank of robbing a pear-tree (a replica, as he doubtless felt it, of the first Fall) is lamented by him precisely as being a 'gratuitous crime'. For Plato and Plotinus the Good was desirable in the same sense as the True and the Beautiful—desirable but not obligatory. We hold indeed the unorthodox opinion that the True and the Beautiful are as necessary to perfected humanity as the Good; but there is perhaps a sense in which they can be left to look after themselves, for in their case men feel no overmastering pull in the contrary direction. Goodness on the other hand—for very many, if not most—needs the aid, as Christians say, of the supernatural, or as modern pragmatists say, of a 'Mythos'. Plato's Form of the Good claims our admiration—though we may sometimes feel, with Wilde, that we would not exchange one of the yellow trumpets of the daffodils for it—but, in the end, it leaves us unmoved. The Platonist 'Fathers', by personalising the idea, by entwining it with our deepest and strongest passions, gave men for good and ill something more than knowledge, namely a 'conscience'; a Freudian, indeed, might see truly in tracing the theology of Original Sin to the sexual lordship of Pagan Patricius over Christian Monica—experienced by the mother-adoring adolescent, Augustine, as a real guilt in the blood. And that sense of urgency, of direction, is near to the mystery of Time: Time, the Heraclitean river—so painfully real to the heart, so unseizable for the brain. Other theologians have said that the world had a beginning in Time; Augustine said better (following Plato) that Time 'began' when the world 'began', and (anticipating Kant) that the human mind creates a Past and a Future. Plotinus, his master in so much, might have taught him that the mind is also its own *place*, and makes its Hell and Heaven; but here the churchman in Augustine triumphed, fatefully, over the metaphysician. There is more, however, to be said in this regard than that Augustine blighted the world with the nightmare of Predestination. Little fault can really be found with his theory of Freedom, as a ratio (roughly) of Grace and the Will—we should say, of Conditions and Character, if under Conditions we include reasons and motives (Conditions alone being prearranged, but Character foreknown, by Omniscience). As psychology, it is surely sounder than the doctrine of his opponent Pelagius, which understressed Conditions, or the later Jansenistic and Calvinistic exaggeration which allowed nothing to Character. Doubtless it appears unjust that though the Elect have enough Freedom to damn themselves, the non-Elect are not necessarily or always granted the Grace needed to save themselves—if we may thus baldly summarise the very entangled doctrine of Augustine, as the Church states and accepts it. But this means no more, after all, than to say that the rich frequently neglect their opportunities —opportunities which might preserve a Eugene Aram from crime. Life, we know, is like that; we can only exclaim with Augustine 'Oh Mystery!' Augustine had seen the sack of Rome—an event as catastrophic to Romans as had been the destruction of the Temple for Hebrews; Freewill was powerless to save the earthly City—only Grace, he felt, could build the heavenly. It seems a paradox that the deep humility of Christian language produced such 'iron men' as Augustine himself, just as the Pauline subjection of Woman was to lead to her dominance in the Romantic conception; but the solution lies in that *willing* Subordination of the 2nd Person—for clearly a voluntary self-denial is the highest testing of the Will. The truth is that the question of 'Freewill' would never have come to the fore but for its association with the doctrine of Eternal Punishment; antiquity knew it not—we today hardly understand its terms. Hell, taken together with Freedom of Action, is bad enough in all conscience—without Freedom of Action it is patently monstrous; and yet, who could maintain that man is ever completely free, or that if he were he could choose damnation? The very fact that we were all 'in' Adam when he fell (for the time, a quite new *organic* conception of humanity), was enough to prove the limits of individual freedom. This was a real dilemma, in which the theologians turned for help now to absolute free choice, now to complete dependence on the Divine Mercy (St Paul's 'freedom from the law'), like souls indeed in hell. One feels that Eternal Punishment was not merely—as no doubt it was largely— a weapon for the conversion of the pagans, a natural if crude analogy with human government, but that (to look deeper) it was a

necessary means for making Man's Self conscious of itself—a
dreadful crucible for the forging of the human Will.

Boethius

DURING THE chaos that followed the fall of Rome, Western man
lived like a captive in a dungeon, awaiting release or judgment
according as the play of Chance and Favour—and a very little
Will—might decide; existence was at best the Immanence of the
seed, the moment between the Decadence of the fruit and the
Transcendence of some dimly hoped-for, supernaturally-con-
ceived, flowering; history itself becomes dream-like and plant-like
—hard for us even now to recapture in imagination. In these
centuries 'philosophy' came to have the sense which it had for the
Stoics (only with a more tragic reality and sincerity), the sense it
still bears in popular speech—the ability, namely, to endure one's
ills with fortitude. Of this mood and moment Boethius's
Consolation of Philosophy is the perfect, the immortal, expression—
even though it might, in no ignoble sense, be called the Philosophy
of Consolation, and although there is also a way to the Divine
through the 'Dark Night of the Soul'. Owing to the absence from
that work of all theological ideas, the writer's orthodoxy has been
impugned; nevertheless the literate few of those ages were
essentially in the right who acclaimed in Boethius a Christian
saint. Only a Roman patrician philosopher could have conceived
the *Consolation*, but only the world-era of struggling Faith could
have engendered it; the accent is not that of Seneca, nor ever of
Socrates. Boethius is an aristocrat of the spirit in captivity to a
barbarian emperor; and the change which had come in the world
has turned his predicament—for his readers and, half-consciously,
for himself—from a personal misfortune into a cosmic symbol.
The lady Philosophy, who comforts the hero with her admonish-
ments, is more than a Muse—she is a minister of Grace and a pre-
figurement of the Beatrice of the *Vita Nuova* (that work so much

reflecting the *Consolation* in its form); the 'goddess' Fortune with the Wheel who plagues him, a familiar motif in the art of the Renaissance, is the symbol of the half-sportive Christian play-instinct—she has not the terrors of the Pagan regents of Fate. From the *Consolation*, moreover, are derived two of the most haunting burdens of European poetry—those expressed in the sentiment of 'Ambition, the last infirmity' and in the nostalgic sigh 'Où sont les neiges d'antan ?' Boethius's more strictly philosophical works show the same elegance of style, and purely philosophic approach, which distinguish the *Consolation*—an urbanity rare in theological works in any age and without parallel in the 6th Century; the doubts which for long were cast on their authorship have now been, for the most part, withdrawn. By his translations of Aristotle's logical works, and his commentaries upon them, he prepared the moulds of language into which the thought of the Scholastics was to flow; and—like Theodoric's capital Ravenna—we think of him as a precious vessel of continuity between the old and the new Rome. He represents the most purely Western element in the later synthesis of the great Schoolmen, as his near-contemporary 'pseudo-Dionysius' constitutes the pure-Oriental: a diminutive Aristotle and an exaggerated Plotinus, the twin tutors of the Christian Early Middle-Age, both of them tenuously Christians.

John Scotus (Erigena)

JOHN SCOTUS is the one pure philosopher of the Ages of Faith—the only one (if we exclude the not very speculative Boethius) for whom philosophy is not a mere 'handmaid' to ecclesiastical dogma: a late descendant, from that island which fable connects with Atlantis, of the long-defunct Alexandrian schools. He is (like many Irishmen) a mystic, but (like most Irish mystics) one of a peculiarly cold and negative sort—a lonely ironical figure, more man-of-letters than saint or monk, type of those 'wandering scholars' (truer 'buffoons of God' than the solemn Franciscans) so vividly

portrayed for us by Helen Waddell. From the point of view of
the later Scholasticism, Erigena falls under the censure of being a
pantheist—a censure which he can scarcely escape. Pantheism, as
Catholic apologists always claim, weakens the sense of moral
freedom and of personality in God—by making Nature divine;
and this, which will not greatly trouble the poet or philosopher, is
no doubt a disadvantage in the realm of action and practical life.
Pantheism (of which the modern names are idealism and monism)
has led—alike as a current in the Eastern or Greek Christianity and
in the secularised Christianity of the West—on the one hand to
subservience to the State, on the other to an unhealthy subjectivism. Against these twin perversions the neo-Thomism of today is
a praiseworthy attempt to build a 'Maginot Line'; only we believe
those old supernaturalist defences will no longer serve. To a
modern psychology, the omnipotence of a personal God and the
infinite responsibility of moral choice would be oppressions,
stultifying action—even if they were tenable for an age which is
nearer in feeling to Erigena than to Aquinas. In John Scotus we
find already in germ the fundamental doctrine of idealism—that
creation (inasmuch as it brings forth 'genera' and 'species') is a
definition, and that the degrees of emanation (as we say, evolution)
from Nothing, and of regression to it, correspond to the processes
of Mind. Thus the question whether God created the world out of
Himself (as the neo-Platonists held) or out of Nothing (as the
Schoolmen were to make a point of faith) turns out to be a dispute
about words only; for God is the Zero which contains all numbers
and their relations, and 'He was not before He made the universe'
—made it, that is to say, by the act of *knowing*. The mystical 'Way
of Negation' first systematised by the pseudo-Dionysius (which
asserts that God can only be defined by negations) becomes, in
Scotus's interpretation, something very like the Hegelian dialectic
—the notion that we ascend the ladder to the One by a series of
affirmations and denials. Thus Life is what is rational and—still
more—non-rational, Being is what is living and—still more—
not-living, Goodness (Erigena's 'One' or God) is Being and—still
more—Not-Being; and it is an apparent contradiction only that,
to Erigena, Evil—as a falling-short or falling-away—is Not-Being.

This argument, which is common to all the medievals and even to 18th Century deists such as Alexander Pope ('Whatever is is right'), will seem to most moderns to be on a par with the schoolboy proof that 'A lie is nothing'; but almost all objection to it should be removed if a clear distinction is made between simple not-Being and negative Being, between Nothing and a Minus Quantity. In this manner the diabolist paradox is avoided (into which post-Reformation mystics and poets such as Blake and Rimbaud—and even philosophers like Hegel—so easily slip) that we approach the nearest to the Good by turning our backs on it, by descending not into 'Limbo' but into Hell itself; the Good of aesthetic contemplation (it should always be insisted) is higher than the Good of ethical action, but is not its denial—they are in a sense contraries, but not logical contradictories. The idealism of Erigena is centred, of course, on God and not upon the human consciousness, and it leaves out almost everything with which a modern psychology would have to deal; he writes solely as an expositor of Christian dogma, but for him there are no Revealed Truths *beyond* reason and, to the scandal of later theologians, he treats Eternal Punishment (that 'most stupid and cruel madness') and the Fall as symbols merely—the one for the soul's entry into the 'Not-Being' of Matter, the other for complacence in Matter's illusions. Worst of all, he is Protestant in tone on the question of transubstantiation —that inversion of the roles of substance and accidents which was to mark the full sundering of reason and the supernatural, the uttermost triumph of what Kierkegaard called 'the Paradox'. That dualism is a still unhealed split in the religious consciousness of Europe, and the Kierkegaardians have re-emphasised rather than healed it; but Erigena was, after all, too much beneath the sway of the neo-Platonist Spirit-Matter dualism, too much in the grip of verbal logic and its antinomies, to be himself the healer. His philosophy was the evening star in Europe's most starless night; but it is not altogether fitted to be the star of morning.

Anselm

ST. ANSELM must be called a most important thinker by his having given the first formulation of the 'Ontological Proof'—the attempt to state in logical terms the intuitional certainty of God felt by all believing (as opposed to merely assenting) Christians. (Briefly, Anselm's argument asserts that—since mind is a reflex of reality—the thought of a Perfect Being implies that Being's existence.) It should be noted that the other traditional proofs—sound, we hold, in so far as they go—do not really establish all that is meant by a God, but only a *metaphysical principle* of causation, necessary being, order, etc. Christian theism—when it is not, as in extreme Protestantism, frankly emotional and non-rational—must stand or fall (as Kant saw) with the Ontological Argument; even if the official-Roman apologetic of Aquinas rejects it, the latter none the less presented it himself in a slightly less challenging form (as the argument, again briefly, that the mind infers the existence of the Perfect from the Imperfect). To those who do not accept the premiss that the Rational is the Real, the Ontological Argument will appear a flagrant piece of sophistry; to those—like ourselves—who accept it, it may still seem unconvincing. And yet, who has not felt, like great Descartes in the 'heated chamber' on that November night that changed Europe, that to have a 'clear and distinct' concept of Perfection is to possess a guarantee that that Perfection—somewhere, somehow—exists? If the clarity and beauty of the argument of Anselm and Descartes fail to satisfy us, it is not that we share the fashionable belief (which the modern world owes, all unacknowledged, to the 13th-Century Schoolmen) in the sole validity of the *a posteriori*; it is simply due to a doubt whether one does ever in fact have a 'clear and distinct' concept of a Perfect Being—whether such a concept is not, upon examination, found to be self-contradictory. The conclusions that really follow from St. Anselm's argument amount to something more like the decried 'pantheism': firstly that this universe—to a timeless spirit—would be perfect, and secondly that a timeless spirit—lacking temporal and spatial existence—would be itself imperfect, would when analysed turn out to be that Nothing which for Erigena was equivalent to Deity, that *Ungrund* which later mystics saw in the heart of Being. It is the tremendous merit of the 'Ontological Proof' to have suggested, in a turn of logic too startlingly simple to be more than an inspired hint, both why the world was created, and why there is that in us which must always claim kinship with the principle of its creation. On the more purely theological plane (no less interesting than the 'rational' one to a philosopher who looks beneath the surface), St. Anselm is equally noteworthy for his theory of the Redemption, which in substance has become the dogma accepted (though not strictly defined) by all Christian churches. Broadly there are three great versions of the doctrine of Atonement which have mingled in the history of Christianity; we may call them the propitiatory, the merely commercial, and the juridical. Firstly, there has been the primitive idea of sacrifice, of yielding the first fruits—as though by an aboriginal *droit de seigneur*, of 'giving back' something—perhaps Everything—to the Fates, of satisfying the mysterious law of Give-and-Take which hangs over gods and men. Second, there is the rather naïve notion, derived chiefly from the popular Judaism, of a ransom—a bargain with the Enemy of Souls whereby his cunning is outwitted and overreached. And thirdly there is the Roman Christian doctrine, first adumbrated by St. Paul, of a substitution—which to the saints has always meant rather an *identification* with the divine victim and exemplar—a harmonisation, however crudely conceived, between the eternal Justice and the eternal Mercy. The second notion, which to the modern reader will chiefly bring echoes of Goethe's *Faust*, was foremost in the sermons of the Fathers down to Anselm, and has an even older genealogy in the mysterious tradition of the Scapegoat. The Devil, it was held, had to be tempted by the 'fruit' of Calvary as he had himself formerly tempted and deluded man with the fruit of Eden, and the greedy villain had—too hastily—swallowed the precious bait, not reflecting that he had no power over a divine subject. This theory—which really makes of every Mass a Black Mass—fell into disrepute after Anselm, but not before it had given rise to the comic Devil (the later Harlequin) of the puppet-plays, the Tarot Fool, the Wandering Jew, the popular

Bad Thief on the cross. Such a figure, the profane analogue of the Crucified Lord—cheated, mocked, in the end affectionately loved —what is he but the bohemian artist of our day, the itinerant circus-clown who has fascinated so many artists? He represents the loneliness in the heart of each of us, the Unknown Martyr— in the army of the martyrs—who has never achieved corporate honour, the ironic nihilism which lives out its doom without either faith or hope. We cannot follow his adventures, which proceed from this point through the heresies and witch-cults rather than in the majestic progress of the Christian Church. To Anselm belongs the credit of defining the other half of the total Complexity —the notion of a Being who, by a more-than-human act of Love, paid a due which mere human Reason and good Will could never pay; a definition which, again, leaves the mind warmed and stimulated, but still questioning. The fable and the chronicle had become 'theology', and the 'Logos' of the Fathers was becoming incarnate in a visible crusading Body; the festival of 'All Souls' was joined to 'All Saints', and (a little later) the doctrinal Corpus Christi added to the scriptural Easter Thursday; the Symbol was no longer static and (as it were) flat, like a Byzantine ikon, but had turned into a 'three-dimensional' medium for thought. The God of the Ontological Syllogism and the God-Man of the Atonement —they represent philosophy's two highest targets, and her noblest failures.

Abelard

MEDIEVAL PARIS,—a huddle of taverns and booths, bawdy-houses with signs hung out in Latin and starving scholars keeping school above stairs, wolves roaming the streets on winter nights, perpetual student-battles during the day—that is the background, only less picturesque than Villon's four centuries later, which has made Peter Abélard and his tragedy a sure prey for the novelists. It has contributed, unfortunately, to the impression that Abélard was a mere quarrelsome loose-living pedagogue, whereas, in fact, he was a man of refinement, great intellectuality (the real founder of what was to be the French style), and—by the standards of most centuries but especially his own—exceptionally pure morals. We may grant, however, that his romance infuses a welcome-enough gust of humanity into the rather dusty annals of the Schools. Of how few philosophers does history enlighten us as to the 'affairs of the heart', if they had any! How few of them have written anything enlightening about an element in existence which was surely not beneath their notice! We think no better of Aquinas for replying— on being asked why he, born of a woman, should shun women— 'Even for that reason because I was born of them'. If Abélard has left us no meditations on the Eternal Feminine—if he was, apparently, unconcerned with psychology in any sense of the word —we may at least fancy it was his French normality and realism that made him successful in marrying the *Name* to the *Thing*. The problem of 'Universals' was, like most medieval problems, a metaphysical question wrongly stated as a logical one; and this wrong 'setting-of-the-question' produced results (as in more sacred matters) which we today are apt to find slightly absurd. (We may well ask, however, if there is less absurdity in the unending contemporary discussion of the 'realist' and the idealist, or in the question—raised by a famous living philosopher—whether the prepositions have an extra-mental reality.) The medieval realist held that a cabbage (say) was a mere imperfect copy of the Cabbage in the Divine Mind; the nominalist, in reaction, maintained that the difference between any two cabbages was absolute—omitting apparently to explain *why* we use the same name in referring to both, why we recognise the word when we hear it a second time, or how in fact we are able to discuss this or any other matter. Each, however, had hold of an important truth, not easy to express in the language of abstraction—a language in which the nominalist was, by the nature of his case, wholly at a disadvantage. It should surely be clear, on the one hand, that the ground-pattern of a cabbage must be laid up—in some indescribable unthinkable manner—in the seed, beyond that—even more unthinkably—in Being itself, and beyond that again—at a point where words utterly fail—

'outside' time and space, prior to all differentiation through accidents of environment. It should be no less apparent, on the other hand, that every cabbage is a unique individuality, which we blur by our merely convenient, approximate, terminology, and grasp only in the immediacy of aesthetic perception. It is by artistic faculty alone that man may perceive both the Pattern and the Uniqueness, may see the Unique as Pattern and the Pattern as Unique, the Name in the Thing and the Thing in the Name; that faculty of 'Imagination' which Blake declared to be 'the copulation of the soul', and which in an era of insensitive logicality—brutal as the tools which scarred Abélard's flesh and spirit—strove for expression in the logic of this lover. His solution—the so-called *conceptualism*—was to derive the Thing from the Thought of God and our human Thoughts from the world of Things; our mental divisions and choppings are a convenience only, due to our human limitation—'one substance is thought of separately from another, but not (properly) as separate from it'. It is obvious that an analysis so nearly touching the mystery of the Trinity must have brought Abélard into trouble—though it was later, virtually, accepted by the official theology; he was accused of treating the Three Persons as Aspects merely, and of thus opening the door to the dreaded pantheism. It is significant that his opponent should have been the famous St. Bernard, the great early-Medieval singer of Divine Love as Abélard was the maimed representative of the Human—two strains later to be distinguished as Cistercian and Courtly Love, and to be united (though with a heavy leaning to the Divine) in the soul of Dante. In that contest it was the genius of humanism, in the person of Abélard, which was broken—the 'Last Father of the Church' was stronger than the first forefather of the Renaissance, the monastery in 'the Vale of Bitterness' stronger than the oratory which he named (as if to mark some new spirit astir) the Church of the Holy Spirit. In Abélard's last letter to Héloïse there is a terrible grandeur, recalling forcibly some letters of another great maimed soul, Jonathan Swift—the extremest tension of that bow of the Will which Christianity, in our interpretation, was sent to tighten: 'In whatsoever place I die I shall leave directions for my body to be conveyed to the Paraclete. Then I shall require prayers, and not tears; then only you shall see me to fortify your piety; and my corpse, more eloquent than myself, will teach you what one loves when one loves a man'.

Joachim of Flore

THE ABBOT OF FLORE is distinguished from most other medieval theologians by his symbolic, almost legendary, character; and, though his doctrines were to be reproved by Bonaventure and Aquinas, Dante in the *Paradiso* sets him in their company. Standing at the change of the millennium—in a remote Calabrian meeting-place of faiths—Joachim announced that Third Dispensation which many have felt to be implied by the Gospel of St. John. His face was turned, not so much towards the sages of antiquity, as to what later came to be called a 'reign of the Saints'—the Kingdom whose promise haunted the 'Spirituals' of the Middle Ages, the later Protestant sectaries, and even the illuministic secret-societies of a more recent date. It is the kingdom of man's Will, successor to pagan Sense and scholastic Reason—that adult autonomy whose chief modern prophet is Kant—always a potency in the future only and necessarily a disruptor in the present. Joachim, in the terms of the great theology, called it the kingdom of the Holy Spirit—the Spirit which, by its very formlessness and ambiguity, seems so often to merge with the Angel that fell, as the Third Realm (in this vision) is preceded by the coming of Antichrist. For the eternal becomes the temporal—with its good and evil—when it conceives a Future; and in like manner the Church has been a seed-bed for that equivocal thing, the modern freed Individual. The individual Will, detached from its origin-and-end, is anarchic Action—in harmony with it, it is aesthetic Contemplation: two concepts combined in the modern cult of the Historical. History is—according as we *see* it as a whole or *live* it in part—the Hegelian masque or the Schopenhauerian shambles. The Joachimian scheme is in fact an anticipation of the Hegelian, without the latter's perilous ambiguity: the Third Kingdom of his conception was a reign of Contemplatives. Joachim's vision, like that of most prophets, was of course foreshortened; the Era which he expected proved to be an Era of Expectation only, the Birth he announced was to be the entry into a painful gestation—it was in fact that negative and chaotic movement vaguely to be known later as Protestantism, and darkened (unprecedentedly) by the illusions of Action. The millennium he foresaw was not to be the millennium of Christianity's 'teens'; *perhaps* we may see a fuller approximation to it in her 'twenties'. It is significant that Joachim's appearance followed directly upon the greatest schism in Christian history—the split between the Eastern 'Orthodoxy' and the Western 'Catholicism' over the *Filioque* controversy; for the definition of the Spirit's 'procession' from the Son as well as from the Father (making the Son, as it were, a second focus of Will) made of the Roman Church, in effect, a Protestant church. The harmonisation of those co-equal Wills, like a re-marriage of East and West, is indeed the problem for metaphysics—as it is for politics—in the coming epoch: the harmonisation which is itself the nature of Spirit or cosmic Will, and the closing of the trinitarian circle. The differences between East and West are still those between absolutist and relativist ways of thought—as we say, between institutionalism and individualism. All this, naturally, was but little worked out by Joachim, who had nothing of the 'immanental' or evolutionary conception which (ultimately) derives from Aristotle; he would seem—it is conjecture merely—to have been associated with the neo-Platonic Amalric of Chartres, and through him to derive perhaps, in part, from John the Scot. More fortunate than the doctor of Chartres, he escaped condemnation during his lifetime; and, in an era which was to make its daily bread of Aristotle, he holds up to us the wine of an older—and later—mysticism, that wine which was to inspire such sweet enthusiasm in the soul of Francis. Like Blake in another century devoted to the Reason, we see him as a mysterious Melchizedek —a minister of the 'Everlasting Gospel', speaking a blessing on the new Age.

Arabians & Jews

DURING THE 'fabulous formless darkness' before the Daybreak in Europe, a civilisation had arisen in the lands conquered by the Crescent, which has seemed to generations of Europeans, only fitly to be characterised by the word 'magic'. It built on no tradition in the past, it laid no foundations for the future—it seems indeed like 'Jerusalem the Golden' of the hymn, a fevered vision of Eternity—riotous with colour and nightingale-song, amidst a desert tract of Time. In these lands (Persia and, later, Spain) the Aristotelian and neo-Platonist writings were preserved—ready to be utilised when civilisation came to Europe—by a line of commentators; but the philosophies of these Arabs and Jews—like the earlier, wilder, constructions of the Gnostics, and unlike those of their Christian successors—remained private, with little relation to the growing needs of popular faith. These writers, if they had laboured in Christendom, would have been persecuted as heretics; in the less philosophic climate of Islam they were merely harassed as freethinkers. The looseness of the Mahometan dogmatic net allowed large 'loop-holes'; and the Semitic temper, which could not admit two Gods, was tolerant of the fancy of two irreconcilable Truths—the theological and the philosophical. Avicenna solved the problem of Universals much as Abélard was later to solve it (by the formula that the Idea is at once *before*, *in* and *after* the Thing—in a word, outside of Time); and Maimonides created a system, like that of Erigena three centuries earlier, both more mystical and more rationalist than the 'plain man's' compromise of Aquinas. The Arabians, however, interest us chiefly by their interpretation of Aristotle's psychology of the Soul—a topic on which the Master had expressed himself with provoking vagueness. The whole question of the 'Soul' was made excessively complicated by the Classical doctrine of Matter and Form—opposites which were held to be related as potency to actuality. It was bad enough that Form was identified with Mind—an identification consonant with the sculpturesque Greek way of thought, but unnatural to the genius of a young religion, to which Mind is potency much more than actuality, a germ rather than a finality. It is perhaps not amiss, in considering an inanimate thing, or even a plant, to identify its 'virtue' with its Form—in the example given by Aristotle, the power-of-cutting with the Form of an edged tool; it is less satisfactory in the case of a man, or even an animal. The latter identification in fact can only be made if by Form we understand a *direction* as well as a *term*—the modern, together with the ancient, sense of the word 'Act'—implying the distinctively human power of conscious Willing; but of this the Greeks, with their lack of a 'time-sense', had no understanding. The matter becomes worse, however, when Christianity seeks to equate the personal 'Soul' with the Form, or the Mind; for the Aristotelian Form was of the class—the general concept—and the Mind was regarded as that Form which is the property of the class of humans. Before this second muddlement the Arabians stopped short; for them the 'Soul' was the Active Intellect, thought of as the last of the neo-Platonic 'emanations' or Aristotelian spirits of the spheres, and associated by them—poetically—with the Moon. Of personal immortality there could be but a shadow—the 'Passive' Intellect—according to Avicenna, or nothing at all—in the version of Averroes. Nor, surely—if the soul is to mean the *rational* faculty—can it rightly be called *personal*; since the reason adds nothing to the 'cognised' object. We today think rather of the 'Soul' (apart from its sense in moral rhetoric) as what is most subjective and non-rational in each of us; by a 'soulless' person we understand an 'unimaginative' one, a prosaic reasoner or calculator. The creative function of *imagination*—so familiar to our ego-centred and 'literary' modern minds—received very little attention in the Classical psychology; it was either lumped with madness ('the lunatic, the lover and the poet . . .') or assimilated to the mere memory—Memory which the Greeks held to be the mother of the Muses. Yet imagination—which creates its own world, which mixes a subjective element with the raw-material of memory and perception—is the one faculty which makes it proper to speak of man as personal or as an image of preternatural powers: the factor which may even be said to give him immortality—if not in his essence, at least in his achievement. The Scholastic equation of man's 'immortal Soul' with his 'specific Form' is, then, a confusion; but it is made still more confounded by the doctrine of Universals which the Schoolmen derived, in part, from the Arabians. The immanent Forms of Aristotle, and even perhaps (though this is more debatable) the transcendent Ideas of Plato, were as manifold as the concepts which the mind is able to educe; the Universals of Avicenna and (later) of Aquinas were solely ideas of species—for no individual could have more than one real or 'substantial' Form. The Law of Contradiction, for the medievals, was rigid; there could be no non-logical or biological 'links'—such as had been at least implied in the organic and relativistic conception of Aristotle. This means that whereas, for the pure Aristotelian, there would have been no real inconsistency in Socrates having the Form 'man' and also the Form 'Socrates' (for 'Socrates' is himself a concept), it was utter contradiction for the Scholastic that Socrates should have an immortal 'Form' all to himself. The contradiction was explained, convincingly or not, by the variously-conditioned Matter of the body—the 'principle of individuation'—destined to be restored to the Soul at the Last Day: a notion which—though it helped to bring the body, and hence the personality, into honour—does nothing to clarify the Soul's subsistence during the interval. The Arabian philosophers, it may be said, set the Crescent in their logical heaven, and rested content in that half-truth; but it was the Christians—seekers for the perfect Round—who found themselves impaled upon its horns.

Roger Bacon

ROGER BACON is the first exponent of the experimental method, and he exhibits in fact that combination of empiricism with an independent spirit which we associate with English genius. Some have even seen in his legendary contests-of-skill with Albertus Magnus the beginnings of Anglo-German rivalry! Fitly perhaps, for the intellectually more considerable Teuton was invariably worsted in these contests. The 'Marvellous Doctor' nevertheless—like many Englishmen—had no lack of philosophy in his bones, if little in his obstinate empirical head; he anticipates by four centuries the great thinkers of the Renaissance, and he is the first philosopher really to conceive the North-European notion of the *individual*—that larva around which the 'Subtle Doctor' Duns Scotus was to weave so dense a cocoon of logic. In Roger Bacon the Classical schema of *Matter and Form* first yields in importance to the—much later—Gothic-Baroque antithesis of *Matter and Force*; reflexion and radiation already dissolve Outline, as in the 17th Century art and physics. With him, for the first time, a body is not moved externally like a croquet-ball by a mallet—rather the 'agent' is a stimulant, releasing the proper activity of the 'patient'; both are successive portions of a single wave of energy. Again, Matter is not, for Roger, poured into Form like a homogeneous liquid into a varied assortment of bottles—'The difference between an ass and a horse is not a difference of form only; it is a difference of matter'. In this he differs not only from Aristotle—as he would have it, from Aristotle's translators—but, interestingly, from that unconscious Hellenist William Blake, with his aesthetic aphorism that 'The only difference between a donkey and a man is in the outline'. 'Substance', for Bacon, has the meaning it bears in common speech today—it means whatever is composed of 'attributes'; it is not (as for Aristotle and Aquinas) a logical abstraction, something distinct from its attributes. He denies, in short, the basic Aristotelian-Thomist doctrine of the (simple and uncompounded) 'substantial form'—a denial with deep implications touching theism which Bacon, for all his boldness, did not draw. The truth is that, by the 13th Century, the logic of Greece had begun to split against the solidity of Fact—as Plato's transcendent idealism had already split on the Petrine rock; and consistent thinkers like David of Dinant and Amalric of Bena were beginning to drive the notion of Matter's *potentiality* into the notion of Deity. The dreaded pantheism, scotched at one point, was reappearing at another—as Alexandrian Gnosticism reared its head in Provence; and Roger Bacon represented a new 'Protestant' plainness as against the cloudy hieratic symbol-world of the Middle

Ages. It may be said that the two temptations of philosophy are the over-exaltation of Matter or of the Ego; if in the old world to brutish natural egoism the philosophers—by reaction—often divinised inert Matter, in our modern world—oppressed by mass and weight—they tend to endow the Ego with an almost 'totalitarian' solitude and irresponsibility. It is worthy of remark that Bacon, the first prophet of materialistic science, is also the first critic of the ancient notion of the unity of Matter; he represents himself as a defender of orthodoxy against pantheistic materialism, and maintains—with a touch of Macchiavellianism—that Matter will be deprived of its sting by being split up. Somewhat similarly, the empiricist Berkeley (like Bacon, a great investigator into optics) professed to disarm Matter by denying it. How ironical that Bacon should have commended his discoveries in chemistry as useful for the war against Antichrist! From this time onward we are aware of that Fear—the 'antithesis' of the Christian 'thesis' of Love—which, like the Arabian Nights' djinn out of the bottle, has ended by projecting its giant image across our era of technology; the fear of that New Man, the *individual*, whom Christianity conceived and carried in its womb.

Bonaventure

BONAVENTURE is the greatest of Catholic mystical theologians, and the controversy still rages around his name of whether he can be rightly charged with 'ontologism'—a doctrine tending not only to mysticism but rather to the disparagement of the 'natural' reason. Ontologism is the belief—deriving from Plato's 'reminiscence', and issuing later in some forms of Protestantism and Cartesianism—that we have knowledge of Things in, or from, God: as opposed to the more modest Catholic-Aristotelian doctrine that we deduce God from Things. For most moderns, it will be necessary to substitute 'the Mind' for 'God' in this discussion—with all the difficulty (still unresolved) of the second position: the difficulty, namely, that we must use the Mind in order to infer its own existence. It should be observed, moreover, that 'the Mind' (otherwise the Self) is almost the opposite of what mystics have meant by God: the modern starting-point and goal is subjective, whereas the Centuries of Faith were arguing about an Object—however intimately sensed. This is the peculiar perplexity that we must be prepared for in comparing the thought of different ages: not only do the terms differ absolutely, but their mutual relation (and therefore most of their meaning) is different also. If for 'God' (in the above dispute) we substitute 'the human Mind', we must further substitute for 'Things' the notion of a 'cosmic order'—and therefore, almost, the notion of God: a difficulty very exactly summed up in the two opposed philosophic senses of the word 'realism'. It is perhaps chiefly for this reason that we find it so hard today to understand Kant, who stood at the midpoint between the two epochs; was he realist or idealist, noumenalist or phenomenalist—where, with him, is the accent laid? He speaks almost in the strain of a mystic about the Thing-in-itself, at the same time as he makes it completely unknowable—in him the tension between the 'I' and the 'Thou' becomes unbearable by the sheer force of his honesty. He felt what no other thinker has yet had the courage to say, a truth deeper than simple pessimism—that we love and crave for something that we can never in fact know. In Bonaventure—and his master Augustine—the problem is, of course, not yet one of *knowledge*, which is assumed; the question as between the Augustinian Platonist and the Aristotelian is roughly the question whether the Creator reveals to us His works (by an 'illumination of the intellect') or whether He is Himself revealed through them—and it seems certain that Bonaventure escapes the 'ontologism' of such thinkers as Malebranche. The Augustinian 'illumination' differs from that of some later 'Illuminists' as the Augustinian 'grace'—already discussed—differs from that of Luther. Bonaventure stresses the transcendental quality of reason, memory and will—which is almost, but *not quite*, to deny (like Kant) the objectivity of space, time and causality; and his suggestion that we could not know the imperfect and limited without some prior knowledge of the perfect and the infinite, however shadowy, is an anticipation *with a difference* of Hegel. Does Nature in effect reveal an uncreate Creator? Does He—do we ourselves—tint the eye-glasses or conjure up a vain show? Does the vision of the world tell us other, stranger, things than the Middle Ages dreamed of? And through what faculty do we receive such—very intermittent—'illumination'? These were questions for a later day—questions which, perhaps, still await men such as Bonaventure and Aquinas were to answer them.

Thomas Aquinas

THE FATHERS of the Church were bishops, administrators, great men of the world; the Scholastics, on the other hand, were monks merely. Especially in dealing with St. Thomas, one remembers that one has to do with a monk—a monk showing the limitations, as well as the peculiar excellences, of his type. If truth has any concern with the complexities of feeling, the tensions of action, with colour, atmosphere and nuance—if it is (as modern art declares) a matter of individual utterance and expression—we shall be apt to see nothing but the logician in Aquinas; the very name indeed, suggests the man, for his work has the clarity, the colourlessness, the impersonal mass and weight, of *aqua pura*. It will be replied that his method is the most perfect reflexion of philosophy's *clartés eternelles*; only, unfortunately, the exclusion of colour is never attained in human words without some sacrifice of light. It would be false to say of St. Thomas—any more than of his contemporary and portrait-drawer, Fra Angelico—that he lacks all warmth of emotion, for his chapters on man's hunger for Beatitude (so astonishing in their omission of all 'psychology'), as also his wonderful Corpus Christi hymns, are vibrant and glowing; but on most other subjects, it must be confessed, the Angelic Doctor's formal manner tends to be irksomely jejune and lifeless. His ethics are less profound than Dante's; his cosmology, lacking the 'poetic truth' of Dante's great allegory, is now little more than lumber; his reasonings on infernal geography—not springing, as in Augustine, from a 'burning' sense of personal guilt—are sheerly repulsive; his pages of double-column objection-and-answer (in which the objections are fairly stated, but the replies often make one wonder whether the Saint really thought them convincing) remind us of the sort of literature handed to their 'yes-men' by the communist and other contemporary factions. Does it appear then that 'Tom of Aquin' can be lightly dismissed? 'We reply, on the contrary', that he is beyond question one of the greatest—greater even than that belated Scholastic Kant, who stands in a somewhat similar relation to the modern era. Paradox though it may sound after what we have said, Thomas's excellence, is, we believe, in the final analysis moral—it lies in the selflessness, like that of any anonymous craftsman of his time, with which he laboured at his massive synthesis of thought and life, reason and faith, of Aristotelian rationalism and Plotinian mysticism; his work, like all the works of the high Middle Ages, represents the attempt to raise into a 'useful art' for all men what in most other periods has been a 'fine art' for the few—an attempt necessarily involving some compromise and rough joinery. Eschewing all literary finesse, and using only the journeyman's tools of the Aristotelian logic, he fashioned the best body of definitions that is perhaps possible for the ultimately-Indefinable—an image and a sign by which all humble journeymen might order their days and tasks. It is indeed true, as Miguel de Unamuno has written, that 'theology which pretends to be rational is nothing but advocacy'; yet a pleader, if he be a philosopher in grain, may hit upon truths which elude a mere cold-blooded inspection. This man, whose modesty would hardly have claimed the title of philosopher or mystic, was led by sheer Love to the sublime affirmation that the End of the universe is 'the good of the Intellect'—an achievement which brings the Saint and pillar of the Church near to another patient builder of syllogisms, the execrated and outcast 'atheistical' Jew Spinoza . . . There are many elements in Thomism over which one might linger, such as its doctrine (nowadays approved by Critical Realists) of *sensible species*, or its antithesis (today hailed—ironically enough—by the Marxists) of Act and Potency; but these theories are more directly Aristotelian, and in this note we can do no more than consider what we take to be its central tenet—the famous Thomistic version of 'Analogy of Being'. It may be said that the tendency of every religion is either to dehumanise the Divinity or to anthropomorphise Him—to make Him either a bare Absolute or all-too-human—to recognise alone in Him, so to say, the 1st or the 2nd member of the Trinity; and it is strictly to anthropomorphise Him to speak of Him as good, as conscious, or even as being (as we understand being). For men who are not mystics such humanisation is scarcely avoidable, yet it lies perilously near to idolatry; the absence, in the education of modern Christians, of any grounding in mystical theory is responsible for the easy scepticism of so many of the educated today. Against all such anthropomorphism Thomas attempts to guard by his doctrine of *degrees of being*; we know *that* God is, but, we know *what* He is only by analogy with various human perfections. Or rather—since He is pure Unity and Transcendence—we must say that He is related to Himself in a way proportionate to a man's relation (e.g.) to his goodness, or his wisdom. In the words of Faust to Gretchen—to paraphrase briefly—'Who can say He *is*? Who could say He is *not*?'. . . . Now a rationalist would have easy work in pulling this construction to bits (while not forgetting that the Saint keeps a corner of Hell for 'irrelevant jokers'). What, indeed, is signified by the misty term 'analogy'? What is it but a combination of the two pre-scientific axioms that 'The effect is like to the cause' and 'The cause is greater than the effect'? There is such a thing as identity—and there is difference—and there is also similarity, which means sharing common predicates; but God has, strictly, no predicates, and if we say He has predicates by analogy we shall have to say the analogy also is analogical, and we shall find ourselves in an 'infinite regress'. And what then was the purpose of those Proofs of God, which surely were meant to establish an actual and not a merely analogical Designer, Unmoved Mover, First Cause, etc. (since the thing designed, etc. is actual)? And passing over this—perhaps debatable—point, what proof have we that the Designer is even analogically good, or the first Cause even analogically wise? There are so many aspects of existence which would suggest a contrary analogy. Would it not seem truer to say (with Job and Kierkegaard) that all analogy between the finite and the Infinite is so distant as to overawe the reason? Analogy is an elastic concept by which we can make divine 'justice' either more than human or (as Aquinas does) a good deal less than divine. The argument that goodness, by the fact that it is good, has more substantiality than evil seems hard to distinguish from the (rejected) Ontological Argument; and if we go on to say its substantiality is an analogy we have proved nothing anyhow. Is not Aquinas really proving God from goodness and goodness from God—the first Cause from Causality and vice versa—and then excusing himself by adding that the relation is 'only a little one'? And, indeed, have such phrases as infinite goodness, infinite wisdom, etc. any meaning at all? Are they not rather contradictions in terms, and would it not be as true—because as senseless—to equate infinite good with infinite evil—or, if one will, with infinite canine-ness—as with infinite wisdom, just as $2 \infty = 4 \infty$? Nor will it help if we drag in this notion of proportionality, for what relationship can be proportional with so singular a conception as the Unknowable's relation to Itself? . . . We have met St. Thomas on his own ground of formal logic; but we hasten to say his luminous intuition is quite unaffected by any such knocking-away (successful or not) of the logical supports. The idea of analogy is in fact a meta-logical one, and the nearest in the whole world of theology to the true nerve of metaphysics; for logic is itself only a guide to truth by analogy with immediate vision. God—if He is to be the Explanation of existence and not just the supreme Mystification—is a term for the inmost relationship of principles, corresponding to the principles within His image or focus Man, of which the Will is the active principle; He is that Absolute which is pure Relativity (or, in human terms, Love); He is, to speak humanly with Aristotle, 'the Thought of thought', but to lean less upon metaphor, the Pattern of which all patterns are isolated figures. It is possible that Thomas was given perception of the idea which our words fumble after, in some wordless manner, at the moment when he ceased abruptly from work—two years before his early death—declaring his great unfinished *Summa* was a small thing compared with what he had seen. It was left for his disciple Dante to express partially in verse —in the vision of the last Canto of the *Paradiso*—what the greatest of religious philosophers failed after all to express—and knew, at the last, he must not try to express—in prose.

Duns Scotus

DUNS SCOTUS stands in somewhat the same relation to Aquinas as does Pascal to Descartes and Kierkegaard to Hegel—with the difference (tending to his under-estimation) that his achievement is almost entirely lacking in biographical or 'literary' interest. This Franciscan might be called the intellectual parent of the Protestant sectaries, as St. Francis was in a sense their spiritual parent—or as the Franciscan order was the true fount of that ultimately disruptive force, European art: notwithstanding that he diminished the sphere of philosophy (as indeed the 'Reformers' themselves were to do) to the benefit of theology. We think of him as a mere logic-chopper, but he used logic—as Kierkegaard used Hegel's dialectic—against itself; like some of the moderns, he was willing, if necessary, to wreck thought and language to express new truth. In spite of his formidable *Systematik* he is the eternal 'existential' critic of System, the 'voluntarist' rebel against a too perfect and imposing intellectualism. It is symbolical of his historic importance that we first hear of him as the defender of the Immaculate Conception: that strictly *metaphysical* miracle, and the dogma through which the earthy associations of the Magna Mater—lingering over from Paganism—were finally overcome. In a similar spirit, Kierkegaard—weighed down by Northern Europe's heredity-'complex'—insisted vehemently, in our late day, on the paradox of the Incarnation. Duns Scotus is chiefly remembered by his assertion of the primacy of Volition—in God and man; though his more daring speculations (the suggestions, for instance, that the Incarnation—as a simple expression of God's

Will—did not absolutely presuppose a Fall or imply an Atonement) are now known to be apocryphal. The history of philosophy may be viewed, broadly speaking, as a contest between the champions of Reason and of Will, the synthesisers and the irrationalists—or as some may be content to put it, the Classicists and the Romanticists. But the argument has always been confused by the unphilosophic 'practical man's' term *free will*; for human freedom consists in the enjoyment of Intellect, and the voluntary principle in man is the animal—the Will is not the positive but the negative element in life, the dark, blind or daemonic force. The confusion springs from the fact that every partial mental synthesis (and no synthesis can be more than partial) becomes a constraint—the garments which are the symbols of man's sovranty are never *quite* made to his measure, and he soon feels himself more unfree even than the naked brute; and this would be true of the 'Omnipotent' Sovran himself, limited by the laws that he has made. Thus when the intellectualist Thomas Aquinas had declared that God wills the Good, Duns Scotus the voluntarist replied that the Good is what God wills; though he did not press the doctrine so far as to maintain, like the interesting medieval nihilist Peter Damien, that the 'Moving Finger' could return and erase the Past, which to a sensitive spirit must be the one 'omnipotency' of any worth—as it is the only intelligible meaning of the orthodox Christian's hope of 'absolution'. The Subtle Doctor should have perceived, however, that Will implies always a discordancy or imperfection —what Boehme called an *Abyss* or breach in primal Being: it aims at Change, and Change must be directed either to a lesser or a greater Good. We should ourselves apply the term Will, primarily, to the former operation—the narrowing rather than the widening turn of the spiral—and call the latter the denial (in some degree) of Will; the hero of action, if he be a true hero, seeks ultimately not Power (or the enlargement of scope for his Will) but the Peace that is Wisdom. Duns saw further than St. Thomas (for the purely rational God of Thomism would have neither the need nor the capacity to create), but his very long-sightedness made him a more dangerous guide; his fallacy is shown in the example he liked to give of a man falling off a precipice—'If while falling he continues to will it, he falls indeed by the necessity of gravity and yet he falls freely'—a true image for the irrational force of Will, but scarcely for Freedom. And we may see a connection between Duns Scotus's emphasis on the Will and his concern with the principle of Individuality—which in the logic-loving Middle Ages was known as the principle of *Individuation*. The question of the Universal—the *quidditas* or 'whatness'—had been solved in a manner by Abélard; but his solution had at once raised another, complementary, question. This was the question of the Singular, named by Duns the *haeccitas*, the 'thisness' or 'whichness': that essentially non-logical or 'existential' problem, from which the almost over-fastidious Greek thought, enamoured of mathematical symmetry, had always turned away. The answer of Aquinas—fitting neatly with his equation of the Universal with Form—was to equate the Individual with Matter; but this really would not do, for the Individual is the Existential, and *pure* Matter could have no existence. And this difficulty St. Thomas must himself have felt, for he preferred to use the rather question-begging phrase 'materia *signata*'—Matter stamped or sealed. Moreover, if the individual is the material, how—Duns pertinently asks—can the soul survive death, when there is no Matter in it? To express his own notion, he employs a language recalling the jargon of our modern art-salons—speaking of the 'horseness' (*equinitas*) of a horse, the 'Socratesness' (*Socratitas*) of Socrates, etc.—a conception which he evidently finds it easier to feel than to define. He comes near to a definition, however, when he states that the term or aim of the Creation is the *person*—neither the body nor (as Aquinas held) the soul, but the *compositum*: and this idea unfortunately leads him and his followers to splutter distinctions without end. But it leads him also to adumbrate a new and very important theory of 'intuitive' as opposed to 'abstractive' knowledge: he insists—in opposition to St. Thomas—that the Intellect has a confused primary intuition of the Singular, darkened only by the accidents of 'its present state', and grounds his thesis (though in a doubtfully authentic work) on the fact that God became an 'individual' in Christ. He urges further that we *love* the individual thing and not the universal, and that love implies knowledge; we have here the very accents of Kierkegaard, though Kierkegaard would have added that 'erotic' love—love as mostly known in the Middle Ages—was love for the 'universal', the 'aesthetic' lure of the Unknown. Beyond this, Duns distinguished more clearly than did any of his predecessors—in his definitions and proofs—between the ideas of Eternity and Time. The Divine Predestination was conceived by him, not merely as prior to human Will, but as it were concurrent with it—the First Cause was not merely the first motion in the Time-Series but, so to say, at the back of the Time-Series; the latter proposition in each case, could be proved by Reason, but the former only known from 'Revelation'. If Aquinas is the last and greatest descendant of Aristotle, Duns Scotus may be called the distant precursor of Kant; they seem like the twin faces of one Janus, or a Gothic gable above a Roman door.

Eckhart

THE GREAT NAME of Eckhart seems to sum up the age of transition from the Middle Ages to the Reformation, much as the figure of Plotinus dominates the one between Hellas and Christian Rome: Eckhart combines a medieval, almost monkish, devotionalism and asceticism with a quite reckless independence of mind, and a tendency to let his excellent pen 'rip'. He may be called, indeed, one of the founders of German philosophic prose, and also the first of that succession of aphoristic thinkers—intuitive rather than systematic, and the despair of mere professors—which includes Nietzsche and Kierkegaard: philosophers for whom Truth is a process rather than a fact, and who accordingly use contradiction, development and 'dialectic' as a method. Such a method seems indeed necessitated by a philosophy for which Time is not (as antiquity held) *merely* an illusion or a derogation from Being, but Being's true form and externalisation: a philosophy which shall be (like the temporal world itself) an image or interpretation of Reality rather than a scientific or logical 'transfer'. Eckhart, as we have indicated, is rich in contradiction; but he is perhaps most truly an originator, and an ancestor of the dynamic-thinking Hegel, in his assertion that 'Before the Creation God was not God'—a Creation which is in fact a *self-cognition*, or differentiation into subject and object, and which takes place in an 'Eternal Now' (that is, at every instant). The Godhead, for Eckhart, is prior even to the triune God: he is, as it were, a Virginhead—a pure Absolute—becoming the 'Father' only in relation to the incessantly-generated 'Son', whom he precedes but also implies (the Son who is the whole intelligible World), as the Unity of zero becomes the Unity of the number-sequence. This is a more vital and activist conception than that of the neo-Platonists, or even than that of Erigena which it resembles; the 'One' of Eckhart is a state of agitated potentiality rather than of rest—a germinating seed rather than a still lake overflowing into separateness at the edges. The idea that the Creator needs or depends on the creature has always—no doubt rightly—been discountenanced by Christian theologians, as derogatory to the divine 'freedom' and as conducive to *hubris*; nevertheless, the definition of God as Three Persons itself binds divinity to its inner relations—relations which are the types of all relations in our world—and primal subjectivity can only be saved by such a scheme as Eckhart's. For Eckhart, the circle in which the Divine eternally produces the Human, and the Human the Divine, must—so to say—rest on a larger circle, like a cone upon its base, or Time poised upon Eternity: and for him the Soul is, or includes, an uncreated portion of Eternity—a spark from the central hearth of Will (the un-grounded 'Ground') instead of being simply (as for Scholasticism) a creature—a reflex of divine Reason. The mystic Eckhart was in fact concerned, like the logician Duns Scotus, to assert the numinous power-and-love aspect of God as against his rational intelligible aspect, upheld by Aquinas; for mankind at this time was becoming aware of the fiery element, no longer merely as the abode of the Devil but as the very principle of Life—an idea which was soon to find expression in the Protestant doctrine of the inner light and the Copernican theory of the central sun. Eckhart is at one with the best 'theosophical' tradition, as opposed to the merely theological, in treating the Supernatural and the Natural, not as wholly separate 'orders', but as analogues or correspondences—in regarding the Trinity not simply as a transcendent mystery but as the very morphology of Reality. Thus man for him, is a supernatural triplicity of Memory, Reason and Will: and a natural triplicity of Apprehension, Feeling and Desire. Such a conception is really at variance with ascetic mysticism, and leads back to the Greek view of the good life as a harmony; and one finds in Eckhart traces of the doctrine—an important one in the Buddhism of the Far East—that to desire God or Blessedness (or even to hate one's past sins) is itself a 'last infirmity', that the truly wise man will wait for Illumination instead of leaving his place in the mighty Pattern to run after it. That he at other times speaks the language of world-renunciation makes him perhaps, as a man and thinker, only the greater; for it was the absence of this note in the later Protestantism, and in the philosophic schools of the 19th Century, which aroused the burning protest of Kierkegaard. The active-souled Western man needs, it seems, more than the Eastern, the directedness of Will and cosmic yearning; yet without the constant re-affirmation of contemplative or 'mystical' values, his Will must lose—with fateful results—its direction. It is for this reason that many of us today look back beyond Hegel—and even Kierkegaard—to the school of Meister Eckhart and to the sages of 'Zen': to 'spiritual poverty' and freedom from concepts, and the eternal Now of the uncreated Ground.

ERRATA

Page	Line	Change from	to
9	21	gramatically	grammatically
11	20	Cero	Zero
29	31	considerably	considerable

DATE DUE